MY
PSYCHIC
JOURNEY

ALSO BY CHRIS DUFRESNE

MY LIFE WITH SYLVIA BROWNE:
A Son Reflects on Life with His Psychic Mother

By Sylvia Browne

ADVENTURES OF A PSYCHIC (with Antoinette May)
ASTROLOGY THROUGH A PSYCHIC'S EYES
BLESSINGS FROM THE OTHER SIDE (with Lindsay Harrison)
CONTACTING YOUR SPIRIT GUIDE (BOOK-WITH-CD)
EXPLORING THE LEVELS OF CREATION (available October 2006)
CONVERSATIONS WITH THE OTHER SIDE
FATHER GOD (available January 2007)
THE HEALING JOURNEY (available October 2007)
HEART AND SOUL card deck
IF YOU COULD SEE WHAT I SEE
A JOURNAL OF LOVE AND HEALING (with Nancy Dufresne)
LIFE ON THE OTHER SIDE (with Lindsay Harrison)
MEDITATIONS
MOTHER GOD
THE OTHER SIDE AND BACK (with Lindsay Harrison)
PAST LIVES, FUTURE HEALING (with Lindsay Harrison)
PRAYERS
PROPHECY (with Lindsay Harrison)
SECRETS & MYSTERIES OF THE WORLD
SYLVIA BROWNE'S BOOK OF ANGELS
SYLVIA BROWNE'S BOOK OF DREAMS (with Lindsay Harrison)
SYLVIA BROWNE'S LESSONS FOR LIFE
VISITS FROM THE AFTERLIFE (with Lindsay Harrison)

All of the above are available at your local bookstore,
or may be ordered by visiting:

Hay House USA: **www.hayhouse.com**®
Hay House Australia: **www.hayhouse.com.au**
Hay House UK: **www.hayhouse.co.uk**
Hay House South Africa: **orders@psdprom.co.za**
Hay House India: **www.hayhouseindia.co.in**

MY
PSYCHIC
JOURNEY

Chris Dufresne

HAY HOUSE, INC.
Carlsbad, California
London • Sydney • Johannesburg
Vancouver • Hong Kong • Mumbai

Published and distributed in the United States by: Hay House, Inc.: www.
hayhouse.com • *Published and distributed in Australia by:* Hay House
Australia Pty. Ltd.: www.hayhouse.com.au • *Published and distributed
in the United Kingdom by:* Hay House UK, Ltd.: www.hayhouse.co.uk
• *Published and distributed in the Republic of South Africa by:* Hay
House SA (Pty), Ltd.: orders@psdprom.co.za • *Distributed in Canada
by:* Raincoast: www.raincoast.com • *Published in India by:* Hay House
Publications (India) Pvt. Ltd.: www.hayhouseindia.co.in • *Distributed in
India by:* Media Star: booksdivision@mediastar.co.in

Editorial supervision: Jill Kramer   •   *Design:* Tricia Breidenthal

Library of Congress Cataloging-in-Publication Data

Dufresne, Chris.
  My psychic journey / Chris Dufresne.
    p. cm.
  ISBN-13: 978-1-4019-0878-2 (tradepaper)
  ISBN-10: 1-4019-0878-0 (tradepaper)
  1. Dufresne, Chris. 2. Psychics--United States--Biography. I. Title.
  BF1027.D76A3 2006
  133.8'092--dc22

                                  2005032217

                    ISBN 13: 978-1-4019-0878-2
                    ISBN 10: 1-4019-0878-0

                    09 08 07 06   4 3 2 1
                    1st printing, May 2006

            Printed in the United States of America

CONTENTS

✗   ✗   ✗

Please Note: All of the stories and case studies in this book are true; however, all names have been changed for confidentiality purposes.

✗   ✗   ✗

The Dreamer
by Sylvia Browne

Come through my door,
O' weaver of schemes,
And you ol' dear,
With many lost dreams.

Come into my room,
Where stories are read,
And let yesterday's sorrows
Lay long and dead.

Come in, young lad
With the world in your eye.
Come in, young maid,
And please don't cry.

The people come through
Young, middle, and old,
And each life a tale,
That has to be told.

To the ear that is bent,
And the heart that is full,
And help is given
To destiny's pull.

Come into my world,
O' dreamer of dreams
Come into my world,
O' schemer of schemes.

There is no one too small,
Nor no one too tall,
That there isn't some grace
From God for all.

Come take the adventure,
Hold bravely my hand,
And we'll all reach together
That far promised land.

Of life now with its struggles,
And with all of its glee,
Let me help you through it,
And in time we'll be free.

The only thing you'll hear,
Is perceptive truth
What I perceive for you,
Will be living proof.

You cannot have cherries,
Without sour cream,
So come into my room
O' dreamer of dreams.

I'm not sure that Christopher, my psychic son, "reads" exactly like I do, but over the 20 years he's been doing readings, people have said that he told them the same thing when also getting a reading from me.

Chris started showing definite, unmistakable signs of being psychic when he was very young, even younger than I was. It was either because he came into it earlier, or after 300 years of psychics in our family we were more aware of it. I don't want to sound prejudiced (but, of course, I am), but from what I've seen of his work, I'm very impressed. I do know that like me, Chris's motto is "Don't ask the question if you don't want to know the answer." He shoots from the hip, with no holds barred.

We don't sit around as many people may think and just be "psychic" with each other. We might discuss a problem that a client has had or is having—but anonymously. The reading room is sacrosanct, and the ethics that we have are true and consistent. We never know our clients ahead of time—they're just names and telephone numbers on our schedule.

Chris has a heart as big as *he* is, all 6'6" of him, and he always has. I hate to admit this, but his patience is greater than mine. Our compassion for our clients runs equally strong, and his philosophy and spirituality are superb. "Oh," you may say, "that's a mother talking." True, but I also value my reputation, ethics, and credibility, and I don't care who he is when it comes to my work for God— he wouldn't be working with me if I felt otherwise.

I know many good and great psychics, but I have to say that as his mother, as a psychic, as the head of a spiritual organization (Society of Novus Spiritus), and as president of the Sylvia Browne Corporation, you'll enjoy and learn from what he has to say, and I guard the authenticity of what we do like a lioness.

God love you—I do,
Sylvia Browne

INTRODUCTION

It was the year I turned 16. I came to my mother's office, as always, and started doing mail-outs, cleaning, and tending to other tasks that no one else wanted to do. . . . Not that I minded, of course. I liked knowing that I was helping, and by this time my friends were starting to admire the fact that my mom, Sylvia Browne, was becoming more famous. And that was fine with me. (It was better than when I was in grade school and the kids made fun of me because they didn't understand, and thought that I was part of a family of witches, fortune-tellers, and worse.)

At any rate, on that Monday in October, my mother interrupted my usual chores and casually ordered me to proceed to the second office—the one next to hers—and start doing readings. I just looked at her and laughed, but my laughter quickly caught in my throat as I realized that she wasn't kidding.

A million thoughts raced through my mind: I could bolt for the door; I could run away and live on the street; or better yet, I could run *in* the street and let a car hit me. But above all, I didn't understand how she could do this to me.

That was about all the time I had for obsessing over my panic as life went from the slow motion of shock to the sudden, unsettling speed of reality. Through my fog of rising terror, I could hear Mom's voice: "You knew this day would come, Chris."

"But not now!" I protested.

"We talked about it."

"Well, you could have warned me."

"If I had, would this be any easier?" Mom asked.

She gave me no time to answer, since her question came as she was shoving me into that second office. "You only have three readings," she said as she closed the door.

Three? It might as well have been 93! Don't get me wrong—like Mom, who was aware of her gift and her lineage by the age of three, I knew from childhood that I was psychic and have always had constant communication with Charley, my spirit guide. My mother and I had talked about my doing readings, and at the time I was excited and thought that it was what I wanted to do, at least temporarily. We'd even discussed the ethics of the reading room, which included the following rules:

- Mom and I were to always tell the person whatever came through, no matter how good or bad. We were just the reporters, not the editors.

- We were to always surround ourselves and our clients with the white light of the Holy Spirit.

- We were to make sure to stress to every client that we're not doctors or God, and we can't and won't control his or her life.

Still, though, as that reading-room door closed, I screamed in my head, *But dear God, not now!* And then I remember a quiet coming over me, followed by a silent question: *Then when?*

The door swung open, and our secretary, Linda, said, "Chris, this is your client, Rita . . . Rita, this is Chris Dufresne." I wish I could give you a few details about that first reading, but to this day, it's still a blur. I just recall that "opening-up" process in my head that's so familiar in my family. Somehow my mouth kept moving, and the client kept nodding in agreement. Then it was over.

And so went the next two readings. . . .

I heard later that all three clients complimented me to my mother and the staff. I didn't hear them because I was too busy sitting alone in that reading room with my head in my arms. I was so glad that those first readings were over, but I was feeling something else stirring in my mind, too . . . could it be elation?

Not only did I get through the readings, I passed the "test." What came out of me wasn't from me—I was just the vehicle through which the information flowed. That realization is still with me to this day, not thanks to false ego, but due to a prayer to do my best and keep the information I pass along as pure as possible.

Did that realization make me less nervous or fearful? Of course not! Nevertheless, I knew that I had helped those three people. Bad news or good, they could go on now with a better map of where they were going and what to avoid. (Make no mistake about it, a legitimate psychic can and will—and does—save lives.) By reading these clients' charts, I was able to advise them about pitfalls and, in a way, put a safety net under them.

Before those "surprise" readings started, I fantasized that the minute I finished, I'd come blasting out of that room in search of my mother, and that in the meantime I'd figure out an appropriate form of torture for her. I was wrong—when I finally did emerge, I still wanted to find her, but not to punish her. Instead, I went to her closed office door and opened it very quietly. She was praying, her hands facing upward and resting on her thighs, her eyes closed. I quickly realized that she was storming heaven with prayers for me—she was as scared for me as I'd been for myself.

I walked in and sat across from her. "Well, Mom, I did it," I announced.

She jerked up and gave me one of those looks of hers, so full of love that it went right to my soul. "I know, son," she said with a smile, "and I'm so proud of you."

I shrugged this off and headed for the door again. "It was no big deal . . . a walk in the park." If there were a hell—which there isn't—I'd surely go there for lying.

Mom was sweet enough to pretend she believed me, replying, "Sure, I knew it would be." I was almost out the door when she added, "And by the way, you have four appointments tomorrow."

So much for my nonchalant act. "What do you mean, 'four appointments tomorrow'?!" I almost screamed at her.

"You didn't think this was a one-shot deal, did you?"

"But . . . it came before I was ready!"

She stood and leveled her eyes at me. "You'll never feel ready—you just do it. Chris, you've always said you wanted to try this, and now you know you can."

"But not like this, not without warning . . . you just . . . threw me in there," I stammered.

"My grandma Ada did it the same way with me," she reminded me. "I know it's hard, but would it have helped if I'd tried to tell you beforehand? You wouldn't have slept—you would've worried yourself silly and worked yourself into a frenzy."

"I *was* in a frenzy!" I pointed out, as if she hadn't already known.

"But you didn't have very long to work yourself up, did you?" She was fighting a smile now. Damn her for knowing me so well and for being right. To this day I still function better if things are sprung on me than if I have time to sit around and obsess about them.

I remember seeing my mom go through her own panic before she did her first live pay-per-view television show, and I understood her agony and hated my inability to do anything about it. In both our cases, when this kind of fear sets in, it's not that we aren't secure about being good at what we do—it's that we want so much to be helpful and to not disappoint those who are standing behind us. We're never insecure about what comes through us, because that has nothing to do with us. But the human part of us wants the people who represent us to be proud of the method, the validity, and the ethics of what we do.

There are psychics out there who do this because "it's a living." That's their choice, and it's not for me to judge. But Mom and I support and are responsible for three major organizations that include numerous ministers, a staff of 15, hundreds of study groups throughout the world, and offices in Seattle and Los Angeles. So we represent far more than just ourselves. It's a joy to do so, but it's certainly also a responsibility that we're proud and conscious of every day of our lives.

There are also psychics out there who exclusively talk to the dead. That's certainly a part of our practice, but we prefer to be more diversified. We have a church, a religious society, and a philosophy that addresses every issue: romance, health (with plenty of medical referrals, because it's important to stress that we're not doctors, nor will we ever pretend to be!), past lives, children, home, marriage, family, friends, and so on.

What puzzles me is, if we psychics can read a client's life chart to explore one area, why is everyone surprised when we're able to read the entire chart? There's no question that people want more and more to be convinced that their departed loved ones made it to the Other Side. But aside from confirming that, they're also anxious to know how to best prepare for the challenges life has in store for them.

It seems important here to explore the fact that departed loved ones don't always want to speak to us. It's not because they've stopped caring; it's just that according to their timetable on the Other Side, you're going to be with them again soon enough. Sometimes communication with spirits on the Other Side is very vivid, while other times it's weak. This depends not on the psychic, but on how strong the soul has become in acclimating to its life at Home. Maybe a client wants to get in touch with her deceased father, but her late mother comes in stronger. I've often seen in my mom's readings that clients will wave away a spirit if it's not whom they specifically asked for, which is a big mistake. Why not listen to whoever shows up? They might have something valuable to say!

I'll act as a medium for departed spirits if it will help a client, but my preference is in reading the client's future and then watching it unfold. No matter how many readings I do, that never ceases to thrill me. I love being validated—not because it proves I'm right, but because it's such an awesome display of God's handiwork and the honor He bestows by using me as a vessel for helpful information. It makes me feel both humble and grateful, and it keeps me going through the pain and suffering this world can put us through.

Even though I know that Earth is really a testing ground for God—a school for learning—I'd have to be as inhuman as a block of cement not to be affected by my clients' suffering: their loss of a child or spouse, incurable illness, broken love affairs, or any of the other countless heartbreaks that pass through my reading room every single day.

I have several goals for this book: (1) to enlighten you so you have a better understanding of what a psychic's life can be like, especially in the reading room; (2) to remove some of the mystique that we're crystal-ball gazers who walk around all day reading everyone's mind; and (3) to help others develop their own innate psychic ability so that through their own powers, they can avoid life's pitfalls, lend a hand to those around them, and—above all—increase their spirituality and communion with God, from Whom all knowledge and power comes.

One final note here: My style is to flow from one subject to the next in an informal, stream-of-consciousness style . . . so I hope you enjoy the ride!

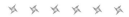

CHAPTER 1

MY BACKGROUND

When Hay House asked me to write about my personal psychic journey as a follow-up to my first book, *My Life with Sylvia Browne*, I have to admit that I was a little apprehensive, not because I have anything to hide, but because it's impossible for me to be objective about myself. But I do think that a little background information might be worthwhile.

There's a 300-year psychic lineage in our family that we can prove. With a few exceptions (like me), this lineage passes through the maternal side—from my psychic mother to my mother's grandmother, Ada Coil (born in 1865); to Ada's mother, Lena Kaufholz (born in the mid-19th century); to Anna Katrina von Bänika (born in 1832). Ida, who was a female doctor and herbalist as well as a reader around 1750, and her mother, Doras, who was also a reader in Germany in the early 1700s, preceded them all. The men—outnumbered though we are—include Paul Coil, who was a medium; Marcus, who was a healer; and Henrich, who was a reader and somewhat of a shaman.

The lineage of integrity and humanitarianism seems just as strong as the psychic one, from everything we've read and learned about our ancestry. And certainly none of us woke up one day and just decided that this is what we'd like to do. We all charted these lives to carry on an equally long line of philosophical and spiritual beliefs. Our heritage is a fascinating combination of German, Russian, and Polish nationalities; and the Lutheran, Episcopalian, Jewish, and Catholic faiths.

But with all my ancestors, spirituality transcends any dogmatic religious upbringing. Aside from being psychic, we all proudly carry and pass along the strong Gnostic Christian philosophy. And while all of us differ in our secondary life themes, most in this family share the primary life theme of humanitarianism. (For more on life themes, please see the aforementioned book, *My Life with Sylvia Browne*.)

People often wonder, by the way, why Mom and I don't share the primary theme of "psychic," as opposed to "humanitarian." The answer is simple: Wouldn't it be redundant for us to choose a life theme to work on that reflects who or what we already are?

I can't honestly say that my childhood seemed particularly strange while I was living it, but again, whatever you're accustomed to tends to be what you consider normal. I remember that there were always strange people lined up all over the house waiting to see Mom, but as far as I was concerned, that's what it was like in everyone's house. Didn't everyone's mother have sessions with all kinds of anxious, emotional people at all hours of the day and night?

I was tortured a bit once I started school because my mom was becoming better known as a psychic. I came home with more than one bloody nose or black eye because someone tried to tease me about my mother being a witch, and I was never known to back off from a fight. My temper and my sense of righteousness have always seemed to block out any fear I might have had of bodily harm. I'm sure that this gave my mother more than one good scare, but as I kept reminding her, at least she didn't raise a coward.

I started "knowing things" as far back as I can remember. I had four "imaginary playmates," which I now know were my spirit guide, my angels, and a few earthbounds (deceased entities who have not crossed over or made the transition to the Other Side). After some research, I've learned that earthbound children will invariably seek out living ones to play with, mostly because children—being among the most psychic creatures on Earth—can see and hear them while the majority of grown-ups can't or won't.

I was also very adept at astral projection and loved to go to the Other Side to play. In fact, when my mother first started describing the Other Side, and especially its Hall of Wisdom, to me, I almost stood up and yelled, "I've seen it, Mom! Just the way you're describing it!"

When you think about it, why do those who have near-death experiences or dreams involving the Other Side all return describing exactly the same landscape? Scientists love to dismiss this phenomenon as a deprivation of oxygen . . . well, if that were true, wouldn't those people have visions of something they could relate to from their own lives, instead of all offering identical descriptions of the Other Side after the fact? Why would Hindus, Christians, Buddhists, Muslims, Jews, Catholics, and so on all see the same exact place if it weren't a fact? It's just too statistically improbable for the identical landscape to be appearing to so many diverse people not to accept sooner or later that we're all going to end up in the very same, very real, Home.

So the work of true psychics or visionaries consists of imparting knowledge of the future, the past, and the present, and also specifics of where we all go when we're finished learning. I believe that in addition to learning, we're all supposed to have as good a time as possible while we're here. It's like a carnival: There are exciting rides, scary rides, and on and on. The objective isn't to judge the rides—it's to just have the courage to take them in the first place and then hang on.

People have asked me if we psychics aren't really just counselors with a flair for the future. Nothing could be further from the truth. Sure, we do spiritual and comfort work, but we'd better be able to give our clients factual information that neither they nor we could possibly know otherwise, or we won't last very long in our chosen work. It's our job to know where a client's sore spots are without them having to tell us, and to give them enough spiritual bandages to help them heal.

I now do most of my readings in our Campbell, California, office or at home, unless I'm on the road with Mom. We travel a lot, from California to New York to Washington to Florida, and we're doing so more and more these days as people become increasingly aware of our work and our honest desire to share our peace, comfort, and spirituality. We record every reading and give the only tape to our clients when it's over. We've heard that there are some well-known psychics who refuse to allow their readings to be taped, and that makes no sense at all to Mom and me—anything we're willing to say we're willing to go on record with, and we even provide the tape recording.

I personally never start a reading without first lighting a candle and asking that the white light of the Holy Spirit surround all of those involved, including me. That serves two purposes: (1) It protects me from any negativity the client might have brought with them; and (2) it assures the clients that we're starting this trip together on pure ground.

Mom and I used to deal exclusively with walk-in clientele, but we've expanded to a lot of phone readings now so that we can work with anyone who needs us, whether we can physically be with them or not. Oddly, sometimes it's almost easier to do phone readings than it is to do one in person, since there are no physical distractions between the two of us; it's just one voice speaking to another. For another thing, there's no reason for phone readings not to be just as accurate as face-to-face ones. Energy is energy, and a life chart is a life chart, even if the client isn't physically present.

It's the same with answering a question about a third person. If a client wants information about his mother or wife, it's easy to read this. In other words, that third person's chart "drops down the chute," so to speak, whenever the psychic reaches for it, no matter who it is.

I've never met a person I *couldn't* read for, but I've certainly had clients who were difficult to read because they insisted on analyzing every word I said, and made it clear from the beginning that they were skeptical and testing me every step of the way. That doesn't make the reading impossible—but it *is* just like walking uphill with a 50-pound bag on your back.

If such people would just relax and listen, they'd hear enough to convince them that I know what I'm doing. It's as if they're more interested in challenging me than they are in letting me help them. This isn't something that happens often, but when it does, I'm always left wondering why they bothered coming to see me in the first place. If people just want to argue, they could easily find someone cheaper and more patient than I am to do it with. When clients come in who are genuinely afraid, I do understand, and it's my job to calm them down—usually by reminding them that all they have to do is sit there while I do all the work, so *I'm* the one who should be nervous.

Anyway, for a few years, I lived in Los Angeles and did my readings from there. But Mom's office was in Campbell, almost six hours north by car, and it was too hard to coordinate schedules, so I eventually moved back to San Jose, just a few short miles from the office. Mom was teaching classes, doing lectures and readings, and training her ministry by then, but somehow we'd both manage to finish at around the same time and spend evenings together.

My days were filled with being a father and a husband and trying to make enough money to support my family; and striving to help my mother, give time to all my clients, and—being a perfectionist—to do it all exactly right. It was at or around that time that my clientele began to grow by leaps and bounds. Like Mom, I hate that people have to wait, so I increased the number of daily readings on my schedule from 12 to 20. I admit that it was exhausting, but like any other workload, when you get yourself set into a determined routine, you're like a racehorse. Twelve clients a day or twenty—it's all part of the same gift that doesn't shut off just because you might be tired. That gift seems to work independently of whatever the physical body is going through.

My work has never been draining. That's not to say that *I* never get drained, but when it happens, my concern is about family, finances, and spending enough time with my children. When I moved farther from the office to a more rural area to give my children breathing room and a more natural place to grow up, the commute obviously began taking even more time away from them, so I decided to start doing most of my readings at home. I converted the den into an office; had an extra phone line installed; invested in a headset, tape recorder and tapes; and I was all set.

Most of the time, it's a dream situation. I love being able to see my children between clients—and William, my seven-year-old son, loves seeing his daddy. Willy is without a doubt the sweetest, happiest, most inquisitive soul in the world. My 12-year-old daughter, Angelia, on the other hand, is smart, loves performing and writing, and is more complicated and tempestuous than her beloved, uncomplicated little brother. Angelia (or Eya, as she refers to herself) is her grandmother's spiritual and temperamental twin.

A typical day starts for me at 6:30 A.M., when I get to spend time with Angelia and Willy before they go to school. I love my children more than life, but I've gone from being a bachelor to being married (now divorced) and fatherhood, and I still sometimes have to stop and try to piece together exactly how that happened. Every once in a while, my mother's words (when my brother and I were very young) come back to haunt me: "This is like living in a damned zoo!"

At any rate, when I finally get the kids off to school, I then disappear into the study and close the door. In quiet, I say a small prayer of protection that my channel be clear and that all negativity be removed from my clients and me and absorbed into the white light of the Holy Spirit.

I will never divulge any client's name, and since I've had thousands of them, I feel confident that no one could ever pick out who's who when I describe readings. I take my clients' privacy and confidentiality as seriously as if I were a priest or a lawyer, and I always will. So, as I talk about these readings, please be assured that they're all accurate and absolutely anonymous (although I have made up some names for them).

The first phone reading starts at 7:30 A.M. On this particular day, it's a woman in Connecticut named Roberta. I start by telling her that she has a problem right above her kidneys, in the adrenal area, and she confirms this. I recommend that she get a complete hormonal work-up, and she says that she's already made an appointment for that exact thing. I also pick up what feels like an ocular migraine above her left eye. Roberta says, "Chris, I've had these migraines for ten years." I urge her to see an eye doctor and be checked for "dry eyes." (I found out later that Roberta did just that, and something called Lacri-Lube did the trick.)

Once I've finished my "health scan" on her, I move on to my client's personal life: "Who's the stocky man with a moustache and glasses, dark hair, a prominent nose, square face, and wearing sideburns?"

She squeals, "That's my husband!" (Notice that I'm not asking her question after question to get her to describe him. *I'm* describing him and simply asking her to confirm. Sometime a name comes, but a detailed description can be just as helpful.)

"Okay, your husband has to take care of his right rotator cuff."

Roberta exclaims, "He had surgery on it last week!"

But I pursue it: "That's all well and good, but watch it because it seems to be inflamed." (Later I found out that he was developing a staph infection.)

I see this man starting a new freelance technical-writing career. Roberta says he's talked about that, but he's afraid, naturally, because like every family man he wants security and stability. I tell her that in ten months he's going to jump into it anyway.

She wants to know how to deal with his tendency to be very internal, and I point out that it's the way he's always been. He hasn't been secretive—he's just keeping his worries to himself so as not to upset her. "You're very emotional," I remind her, "so he's protecting you."

"Oh," my client replies, "I never thought of that."

Now I get a vision of a small boy, somewhat frail looking, dark haired, and small boned: a son who needs to be checked for an iron deficiency. I really emphasize this, because now I'm very concerned for the child and want Roberta to take this seriously. She's suddenly nervous, but she promises to take him to a doctor—better that she gets nervous than her son becoming dangerously ill.

I now "see" an older woman whose life is coming to an end. I describe the woman to Roberta, telling her what I see. I hear a gasp, and then in a small voice she says, "Chris, I felt that my mother's time was coming, but she's given up." She begins to cry. "I'm glad you told me so that I can prepare." (As an added note, I should point out that I'm sure people know these things on some level more often than they give themselves credit for.)

Next, my client and I get into redecorating a house and buying some land. We also talk about other relatives, including a brother who drinks, and I can't see it stopping—so it does no good for her to try to save him, because he won't admit he has a problem. I tap in to the presence of an entity—in this case, Roberta's spirit guide is there, as are two angels, but there's also an older man who died of a stomach ulcer that bled out. She excitedly tells me, "That's my dad!"

When the reading ends, I bless my client and promise to send the tape of her reading as soon as possible. We hang up, and I sit there quietly for a minute, regrouping, and labeling her tape.

Then the headset is back on, the tape is in the deck, and the next client is on the line. It only takes a moment before I realize that this woman, Gabrielle, is hysterical. As she sobs, I start silently racing through every possible scenario and quickly get it: a furry animal . . . a cat. "You've lost your cat."

She cries, "Yes!" Now I'm an animal lover, but I'm not having any success calming her down, and I already know that her cat is dead. I go into the fact that all of our animals are alive and well on the Other Side . . . and then it comes in strong and clear that this cat has been dead for 14 years. I never judge anyone, but sometimes you have to get a little tougher, if for no other reason than to attach rationality to an emotion that's out of control. I tell Gabrielle that she should see her doctor or a psychiatrist to help her work through her grief.

"Get another cat," I advise. This seems to strike a welcome chord. More philosophy, and then we discuss a trip that I tell her she's going to be taking with her sister. Gabrielle hates her sister, but she says that she'll consider it.

This reading wrings me out a bit—but instead of taking a break, I go right on to the next one. Sometimes when you get on a roll, you have to ride it out. So I dial the next number, ignoring a vague realization that I haven't eaten in hours. This client is named Joyce, and she likes to chat. After 20 minutes, I quit trying to outtalk her. I'm very conscientious about people getting their money's worth, and I remember something my mom once told me: "Clients hear what they need to hear, and sometimes they just need to vent." I prefer good listeners, of course, but I really don't mind the talkers. The only clients I find difficult are the ones who automatically say "No!" and want to argue with everything I tell them. Invariably I'll get a letter from them a few weeks or months later saying, "You were right—I just couldn't see it then."

I inherited Mom's passion for researching all facets of the paranormal, and someday when I have extra time and resources, I want to look into why the results of some clients' readings are more immediate than others. I know that we each write our own charts before we come here, but it's fascinating how you can tell one client about something that happens the very next month, while others have to wait for years. Like my mother, I never, ever lie to my clients, so if they have a period of four months or four years—or ten years—ahead of them before an event they're waiting for comes to pass, that's exactly what I'll tell them.

Believe it or not, it's almost as aggravating for me as it is for them when they have to wait so long. Our lives move in cycles of active periods, dead periods, periods of sorrow, periods of joy, and so on. I always feel bad for clients who're just starting a long survival period, and I have to explain that it's not going to be over quickly. But at least I can assure them that sooner or later it will end, as those rough times always do for all of us.

A client recently said to me at the end of a reading, "Well, Chris, I guess I have a really boring life." As I told her, it depends on how you look at it. Even if you're very rich or famous, you still have to eat, sleep, shower, comb your hair, have your teeth cleaned, shop, and what have you. Everyone's lives, even those of celebrities, get humdrum from time to time, if not downright exhausting.

Take Mom, for example. She doesn't think of herself as a celebrity, but since she gets mobbed everywhere she goes, I'd say that she qualifies as one. Just as an example, she lectured in 66 cities in 1999 to promote her books, did 14 episodes of *The Montel Williams Show* and two pay-per-views for cable, in addition to keeping up her nonstop reading schedule, taking care of her church and office, plus all of her police and charity work—not to mention making sure to spend time with her family. And people want to know why I don't want to live more in the limelight?! How glamorous is her schedule when you really look at it? It wears me out just watching her, and I'm 39 and she's 69!

But I guess it's in our blood—after all, my great-grandmother did readings until she was 89 years old. Her mother and brother were 94 and 96, respectively, when they finally quit doing readings, and even then it was only for a perfectly good reason: They died.

There's no question that doing readings at home is a little slower than doing them at the office. I'm pretty disciplined, but I can't resist sneaking out to check on the gardener, grab a Diet Coke, and help myself to a bite or two of chicken before I head back inside and close the door again.

People constantly ask how I can do readings over the phone. "Do you see me?" is a common question. The answer is, "Yes, but it's your *life* that's important!"

"What do I look like?" is a pop quiz I frequently get, and it's a waste of valuable time.

"You're short with dark, curly hair; a pouty mouth; blue eyes; and a rounded figure."

"Wow, Chris, that's exactly right!"

I already know that. I stifle a sigh and hope that I don't sound impatient when I say, "Now can we go on, please?"

Again, I start with health, then family, relationships, career, finances, and so forth, and finally we move on to any other questions the client has. The same faculty that works face-to-face works over the phone. A chart is a chart, and it all comes from God. It doesn't mater where you are, He will still drop the chart down for me to see. I've even had clients give me a false name. It doesn't matter—it still works. You can fool Chris, but you can't fool God.

One thing that Mom and I have talked about extensively is how readings often share common themes. She obsessed about that for years and has come to realize that in the grand scheme of things, people in the same circumstance will tend to group together.

For instance, I'll have a day when maybe 70 percent of my readings are with individuals who are getting a divorce. Another day, at least 50 percent of my clients have a parent who has just passed away. Two days in a row I had nothing but clients who'd lost either jewelry or a pet. It's as if a silent signal goes out and everyone who has the same problem that week or day or month books a reading. Our staff certainly doesn't schedule it that way, because all they deal with is the date and time when the reading will happen.

Some days are all death and dying or missing children, and that's hard. Of course, as far as I'm concerned, each question is important and every problem is critical—all of my clients deserve my undivided attention and my clearest mind so that I don't start accidentally reading myself into their lives. My ego has no place in a reading, and I can't read to get kudos and compliments about how right I am, because again, it's not coming from me. I'm there to give comfort, protection, insight, and advice to help my clients understand the themes of their inevitable hard times, so they can then see what they were meant to learn and measure their progress toward that goal.

The hardest emotion to deal with is despair, because typically this means that dark forces have invaded just enough to compromise spirituality and faith in God, leaving the client in a state of hopelessness, loss, and grief. I consider it part of my sacred responsibility to help those clients restore their belief in their Divine connection to God and their awareness that none of us is ever alone, along with their pride and sense of well-being.

I can't tell you how much harder it makes my job (and, of course, Mom's, too) that there are so many phonies out there who milk people for information and then simply feed it back to them—actually charging them for what boils down to just a cheap trick. What keeps me from getting too discouraged is how convinced I am that honesty and integrity will ultimately win out. I've seen my mother prove this over and over again, like when she turned down an offer of $40,000 to sponsor a psychic hotline, even though we needed the money. But if you compromise your ethics even once in your career, marriage, family, or friendships, you're headed for disaster. The karmic price of that kind of compromise is much too high to pay.

It's interesting to me that the most successful of the businesspeople I talk to are the ones who, when I tell them their best opportunities for growth in whatever business they're in, say to me, "Oh, Chris, that's exactly what I was thinking, but I needed confirmation." This is additional proof that everyone is more psychic—including about their own lives—than they give themselves credit for.

Back to the day I've been describing. Readings are over, and Willy comes running back to the reading room, yelling, "Daddy, work no more!" in his deep, raspy little voice. Angelia comes in and crawls up on top of me until she's literally sitting on my neck.

"Where do you want to eat?" I ask.

I don't have to be psychic to know what the answer is going to be. A loud chorus, in unison, cries, "Benihana!" Their favorite is a Japanese restaurant we all love, but they want Bagdah (their name for my mom) to come, too. I remind them that she can't, since she's traveling again.

"How long this time?" they ask.

"Nineteen days."

Angelia's eyes fill up. "I miss her, Daddy."

"We all do, Eya, but Bagdah has to get out there and promote her book and her church." My daughter nods—it's a simple statement of fact we all realized and came to terms with years ago.

The kids and I end up going out for sushi near our house. They eat like horses—you'd think we never fed them! Willy is shoveling his food in his mouth so fast it looks as if he's afraid someone's going to take it away from him. I glance at the clock on the drive home and can't believe it's almost 8:30 P.M.

We hurry home. Angelia finishes her homework, and it's time for her bath, and then into bed for story time. This isn't reading from books, either—bedtime stories have to be original, and Angelia and Willy have to be the main characters. Mom once told Willy a story about him being a pirate, and ever since, no matter what other tale I feel like telling, he gives me a frown and says, "I want a pirate story, Daddy."

Finally, everything is calm. I settle in to watch the news, grateful to have a couple of hours alone, and suddenly it's 2 A.M. I've fallen asleep with the TV on. So much for those cherished couple of hours. But, oh well . . . it's hard to find time for myself, but I'm sure it's going to be harder in a different way when the house is quiet someday and no one needs me there constantly to be their daddy. Being the youngest, I was the last to leave my home, and I remember the forced smile on my mother's face when it was time for me to go—as if I couldn't see through it to the sadness in those huge brown eyes of hers, which are as readable as a giant billboard.

We live three minutes from Mom now, and we all love being with her. I'm selfishly glad that she had more time than usual to spend with me when I was 14, when my psychic gifts were beginning to gel hard and fast and she could guide me and quell my fears about what I was feeling and seeing.

My gifts coming to fruition at the same time that puberty hit—while I was stuck being a male with my testosterone running wild—only complicated things. I remember a particular time when I found out that one of my first loves had cheated on me with another guy. I was so devastated that I asked my mom, "How can people be so mean and disloyal and hurtful and deceptive?"

She looked deep into my eyes and said something I've never forgotten: "Chris, I've asked my grandmother and Francine [her spirit guide] the same thing again and again, and the answer keeps coming back: 'Unless we can experience great sorrow, we can't help other people.' We have to know pain so that we can ride that dark horse with them, down into the deepest labyrinths of their minds."

To this day, when darkness hits, I remind myself of that conversation and of the fact that just like everyone else, I have to learn for my own soul's perfection.

THE PSYCHIC GIFT

Skeptics say that visiting psychics is a pursuit of the weak. Well, if that's true, then I'm convinced that those skeptics would have to say the same thing about practicing religious beliefs as well. You see, we legitimate psychics aren't just visionaries—we're people born with a gift from God and a direct philosophy that's absolutely Christian (although all religions are covered by the loving umbrella of Gnosticism that my mother and I practice).

I've asked myself many times if I would have embraced the Gnostic philosophy and my reading work if it hadn't been for Mom. I can honestly say that while I might have made the mistake of waiting longer than I did, I would have found my way to all this on my own. I might be a tough nut to crack, but you can't argue with logic, caring, and a loving God. Even the greatest minds on Earth share the simplicity of the belief in this strong, constant, eternal light shining on the soul.

The way my mother kind of sprang this career on me without warning seemed like a dirty trick at the time, but I can see now how smart she was to handle it that way with me, and I'll always be incredibly grateful to her for it. As I said on her second televised pay-per-view, to be able to help someone find that one part of themselves, that missing link between them and their Divine birthright, to help fill in the lonely spaces with truth and then to see their eyes register and recognize that truth . . . that is truly as good as it gets.

I've been asked a million times how this works, how we do it. I've spent countless hours thinking about the way to answer those questions, and I believe that it's harder to explain when you're born with this gift, because there's nothing to compare it to and no way to know what it's like *not* to be psychic . . . so I can better describe what it *is* like. All I can do is live it.

Mom and I are teachers by nature, so nothing would please me more than to give you the key to our own abilities. Nothing in the psychic area should be hidden or secretive because that can only lead to occultism. It should never be a guessing game, where you provide more answers than the psychic does. Feedback helps, but only to validate what's been relayed to the client.

The best readings happen with people who are open and at least somewhat conversational. It's not that you won't get a perfectly good reading if you come in with a negative attitude, but you're bound to get an even better one by simply being nice. Just like everyone else, the more acknowledged and appreciated we feel, the more effective we're likely to be. We psychics are human beings, after all, and we have feelings. Sure, you're paying us to help you, but we also really *want* to help you, more than you could know.

At any rate, let's get into the process, and please bear with me as I try to explain the difference between feelings and certainty. Some of this will overlap, but I'll do my best to be as definitive as possible.

Feelings are an intuition, a sometimes-vague sense about something. They start out something like this: "I don't know why I don't like this [car, person, house, or whatnot], but I don't." We might try to rationalize it later, but there's no logic involved.

The psychic sense, however, starts out with a feeling that grows almost immediately into a resounding yes or no, but with the reason, logic, and language that go with it. In other words, it becomes explainable: "I don't like this house because not only is its energy incompatible with me, but it seems that there was some kind of trauma here between a man and a woman, and that negativity still lingers."

Sometimes the psychic information stops there. But very often, it goes further: "This house is not good for me. I'm sure that the land it was built on was the site of a war between Native Americans and white settlers, and many people were killed here. There are two spirits inhabiting the house now—an older woman and a young girl named Hannah."

That exact scenario, with a lot of added details, was played out recently with a client of mine named Marisol. She validated everything I told her by confirming that she'd seen a young spirit girl on her property whose dress was very simple, conservative, and Amish looking, from what she described.

The more you explore your mind when those first images start coming and push your false ego out of the way, the more you'll be infused with ever-greater clarity. Don't get frustrated if this openness is gradual in coming—when

I started out, I was somewhat slower, too. It's natural to have to work up to exercising the new "muscle" of your psychic ability.

Like my mother, I begin every reading by stressing to a client that I'm not a doctor or a psychologist—I'm really a reporter. God and the client are the editors who wrote the client's life's chart before he or she was born into this lifetime. If you find yourself doubting that, just think about it . . . if you didn't have a chart, how could anyone do a reading for you? What would they read? And if we didn't all come here with a plan, what would be the use of all this? Never forget one absolute fact: *The reason we're here is to perfect ourselves for God.* It's that simple, and it's that amazing.

I find that most people don't fail to plan—they plan to fail. But you can't totally fail *your* plan. We each *live* our plan, but the idea is to embrace the knowledge we've gained afterward into our soul when we're Home again. Each and every one of us has a right to feel great pride in just the accomplishment of living. The only way to fail is to give in to despair or fall into the trap of suicide—which is the ultimate act of dropping out of this tough but worthwhile school called life on Earth.

The first question I ask myself—not my client—in every reading is, *How is his or her health?* I didn't know human anatomy when I started doing readings as I do now, but I've always related whatever answer I got to that initial question. "Left side, lower quadrant of the stomach," I might say, and if I couldn't *name* the problem spot, I could certainly point to it.

Again, I'll always urge everyone with a health problem to see a doctor, but when I get a strong image, I will give advice—as I did the other day with a client named Jocelyn. I told her to eat more roughage, because I could feel that her intestinal area was stuffed and clogged. She nodded, and agreed that that area had always been a problem. I also recommended natural vegetable-enzyme tablets, and I heard later that the problem was cured.

On the other hand, what if Jocelyn had shaken her head and said that she was having no trouble in her intestinal area at all? It used to throw me when that happened, as it still sometimes does. But I finally realized that I was seeing into the future, to a problem that was going to develop that she could guard against by taking preventive measures now. Many clients have said, "Chris, I just knew that you were wrong, until my [liver, gall bladder, stomach, or other area] started giving me trouble a few weeks [or months] after my reading."

So, I always tell clients, "It's fine if you say no, but please don't completely disregard what I tell you; just have it checked. After all, it's better to be safe than sorry."

CHAPTER 3

GUIDANCE
AND ACCURACY

One question that clients often ask is: "If my chart is already set before I come into this lifetime, then how can you or anyone intervene?" I always reply, "I was probably written into your chart for the same reason that you were written into mine—so that I could give you a warning signal along the way."

For example, let's say that you're driving from Los Angeles to New York. You have the map laid out, and you've planned out your rest stops, eating places, and where you're going to spend the night along the way. But once you're on the trip, there might be traffic, roadblocks, and bad weather, and someone in a yellow raincoat may unexpectedly advise you to take a detour because the bridge is washed out ahead. You're still going to get to your destination, but it would have been a lot tougher without that helpful person in the raincoat alerting you to an unforeseen problem around the next bend.

Along with me and all the other people written into your chart to help you if you start to wander off course, there are spirit guides and angels watching over you as well. These helpers serve a role similar to a music conductor: No matter how skilled a symphony's musicians are, or how beautiful the music, a gifted conductor coordinates everything and makes it flow smoothly and perfectly.

Likewise, my mother and I can and will only *advise* you. You should be wary of anyone who wants to control you or encourage you to come back to them time and time again. I don't mind repeat clients, but the last thing I want is for someone to become dependent on me.

Once the health issues have been resolved in a reading, the next question I ask myself about the client is: *How are their personal relationships?* This is often the highest-priority area for clients and comprises about 90 percent of the problems that they bring me. People of every age, even when they're very ill physically, still start out asking about Mr. or Ms. Right. Believe me, I'm not condemning this. It's just a simple fact: Love does make the world go 'round—as it should—because God, after all, *is* love. So really it's a manifestation of exactly why we came here.

Romance is also very often the most troublesome area for a psychic to deal with, because heaven forbid that you don't see who a client wants you to—that love interest they have their heart set on. When that happens, I usually only get one response from the client: "You're wrong!" And if I don't hear that, I'm likely to get: "Can't you change that?" It's a guaranteed argument if I tell a client that the person she's in love with isn't who she'll end up with, or that his marriage will end when he hasn't yet realized that divorce will be a good thing for both parties in the long run.

No psychic, including me, is accurate 100 percent of the time, but we'd better be right more often than not or our careers will be short ones. And when we do describe Mr. or Ms. Right down to the most minute detail, it's very likely that we're then going to be asked for the person's name, city, street address, and—if we haven't already managed to change the subject—his or her phone number!

I do understand—and I mean no disrespect—but please, give me a break! When you've described someone all the way down to a gnat's eyebrow, and have explained when the client will meet him or her and in what setting, you'd think that would be enough!

Just the other day I got a letter from a woman named Isabella whom I did a reading for a year ago in which I managed to come up with Mr. Right's first name. She reported, "Chris, I met a man in September, just as you said. He fits your description to a T, except you said that his name would be Jesse, but this man is Jess. . . . Could they be the same person?" I'll leave it to the reader to imagine how I felt and what thoughts flashed through my mind.

CHAPTER 4

A DAY AT THE OFFICE

When I'm not working at home, I'm doing readings at the office. I hope that I can give you a good idea of what a day in our office is like. Mom and I often said that the reality of it would seem like complete fiction or the plot of a terrific sitcom if we ever really tried to describe it to an outsider.

I typically arrive at the office around 8:30 A.M. to find the place already buzzing with the regular staff, the ministers who are on duty that day, and any number of volunteers—there are often 20 people or more energetically dashing around. It's interesting to note that most of the "regulars" have been with us for 27 years, while the average "newcomer" has been around for about 16.

I disappear into my room, and our appointment secretary, Michael, shows up momentarily with my usual Diet Coke. The phones go on automatically at 9:00 A.M., and then callback lists are getting compiled and faxes and e-mails are flying off to our Seattle office. Our product manager, Darren, is packing boxes for an upcoming lecture, making sure that all printed materials and supplies are included, while Michael is finishing every last detail of some very complicated travel arrangements for Mom and those on the staff who are accompanying her. Our trusty business operations manager, Linda, dashes in with my agenda for the day, which includes issues that require immediate attention. An emergency case needs me to fit her in if at all possible . . . there goes my lunch hour.

I hear my mother come in. The staff line up with questions for her, starting with, "A client wants to know if her foot surgery can be put off."

After a quick conference with the woman's doctor, Mom answers, "Yes, no problem."

Two new murder cases have been faxed in, and someone asks, "When can you get to them?"

There's regret in Mom's voice when she says, "As soon as I take care of the 55 cases ahead of them."

Linda brings a huge stack of letters for me and wonders if I want them on my desk or in my car. Definitely my car—I can't deal with them now.

Every phone line is lit up. Some of the staff members are retrieving voice mails, some are returning calls, and others are answering new ones. I can hear the whir of the tape recorders in the back room. Mom tells Pam, the office manager, that she needs the tape about the Winchester Mystery House investigation. Michael retrieves it from the cabinets filled with categorized audio- and videotapes; affidavits; police cases, both solved and ongoing; inquiries, both answered and pending; validations by the thousands; and more thank-you notes than we can count.

I hear Mom close her office door. She's beginning her day's readings, and I start to tackle my first three. By the time I emerge again, the mail has arrived in huge crates. Pam, Linda, and Michael are sorting it all. Mary, another staff member, takes the letters with questions; Linda deals with bills, business, and junk mail; and Darren handles the product orders.

About this time, three people walk in and exclaim, "Is this really the place?!" We confirm that yes, it is. They browse around and buy some products. A woman is in the corner, silently reading.

Michael meets Mom in the reception area and starts reviewing her upcoming appearance schedule while she just looks at him with a dazed expression on her face. I innocently eavesdrop and hear that we have two filmings at Mom's house: *People* magazine and the *Montel* show want remote shoots with Mom and me. I'll do it, of course, but I've been through enough of them to know that one hour of footage means four or five hours of work.

Michael announces that the printer's down. No wonder—it never stops. Linda tells him to get the job to an outside printer ASAP: We have a deadline. During that scene, two more staff members, Gene and Vera, stagger in with orders along with the mail carrier, who manages a wan smile. Then four more people wander in, just as the UPS driver arrives with a package and flowers.

Suddenly, my mother bursts out of her office, clearly not happy. "I've got another blocked number!" Pam mutters a curse, and assures her that she'd told the client to remove the block so that the call could go through. Linda offers Mom some tea and asks if a young girl in the reception area can have a photo with her, which Mom agrees to.

It's getting close to lunch. Michael takes orders and dashes off to KFC to bring back our food, and a meeting is convened in our conference room about overhead expenses, salons, classes, and upcoming travel itineraries.

Mom says, "I'll take on more readings—so will Chris—and God will provide. He always does."

Classes are starting soon, and the ministers are ramping up to teach four nights a week at the community center. Mom makes out the schedule while Linda writes it down in shorthand. Then my mother and I open and answer as much of our private mail as we can before our next readings start.

Meanwhile, Michael is fielding media calls, and Linda is working on figuring our retail-sales tax, payroll, rent, phone bills, and other office expenses, in addition to doing the daily bookkeeping. In between answering calls, Vera is responding to e-mails, while Pam is finishing labeling our readings' tapes before the afternoon mail goes out.

I hear a shout. For the thousandth time it occurs to me that we have a very expensive intercom system, but Mom has never used it—yelling is easier.

Michael is trying to rearrange the library, and Tom is making sure that the video camera is in working order for that night's ministers' meeting. I can't stay, though—my daughter is in a play.

The phones shut off at 5:00 P.M., but no one leaves. There are still flyers to be sent out, and Darren has to update the Website about the venues of Mom's upcoming appearances.

After Angelia's play, I have a few hours to write before I collapse into bed. Some days are calmer than others, but it's still full speed ahead every minute.

We're so lucky and so grateful. Everyone in the office is so committed to God and their own personal belief system that even on the rare occasions when personality differences crop up, we can still work together effectively. I know beyond a shadow of a doubt that when people have a pure, honest motive that's greater than they are—for the betterment of the world—their work becomes a stimulating, gratifying lifestyle. At least once a day I hear someone say, "I love it here!" And I always think, *Me, too.*

People who walk in off the street and clients who arrive for in-person readings always remark about the positive energy in the office and the warmth and love they feel among us. It's not an act, believe me. We don't have any interest in pretense, let alone time for it. Our belief system contains no dogma, no recruitment, no shoving anything down anyone's throat. In fact, we have the utmost respect for the reality that what you believe is *your* truth, especially if it brings you joy and the ability to live with the knowledge of a loving God. What you put out there, you get back, and if you love God and treat His children well, He'll take care of you.

We also have a very active prayer group that's a true blessing. We take names from callers all day long, which are then forwarded to our hundreds of study groups and our ministers, who pass them on to the prayer line. The result is that every night at 9 o'clock, thousands of people pray for those names on the prayer-chain list. Imagine how powerful that is!

We're also blessed with tireless ministers who give spiritual counseling on the phone every Sunday and Wednesday. They visit nursing homes, hospitals, and shut-ins;

officiate at weddings and funerals; and act as liaisons between the office and our study groups, which now span the United States, as well as other countries all over the world. The ministers also help compile research material from our trances, lectures, and past-life regressions, filing and cross-referencing them on computer disks along with Mom's other 50 years of data. And during the holidays, the ministers and volunteers gather and distribute truckloads of food and clothing for the poor.

I don't know what other psychics do with their money, but I'm willing to bet that none of them support all the organizations that my mother does. Someone asked Mom not long ago if she realized how rich she'd be if she didn't funnel so much of her income into her spiritual and humanitarian works. She answered, "Yes, but what else would I do?"

My mother and I are very superstitious in a way. We believe that if we didn't share these gifts we've been given and put them to work for as much of humankind as possible, we could lose them. Does that make us noble? Not at all. To be honest, we're almost selfish about the satisfaction and pleasure we get from our efforts to bring comfort and spirituality to the lives that we're privileged to touch. How empty life would be without a commitment to a greater good than just one's own bank account!

CHAPTER 5

ENTITIES
AND ENERGY

A client recently asked me how I feel about *Ouija* boards. This feels like a perfect opportunity to warn you to stay away from them.

It's not that they don't work—it's that they provide usually earthbound spirits with a vehicle whereby they can lure you in at the start with a little valid information, and then once they have your attention, wreak havoc on your life with all kinds of crazy and untrue messages. Earthbounds are very opportunistic—when you sit down at a *Ouija* board, you open the door to any number of spirits who aren't at peace. They interpret your willingness to "play" on the *Ouija* board as an indication of sympathy and welcomeness toward them that they feel free to take advantage of. . . . So why expose yourself to entities who (to say the least) don't have your best interests at heart?

Don't get me wrong . . . I've never been afraid of spirits who've passed away, earthbound or otherwise—it's the living who can be more of a threat. But in general, no matter where negativity is found, whether in the deceased, the living, or even in objects, the battle against it is an ongoing one. Rather than trying to ignore or deny its existence, whenever you run across evil in any form, bless it with the spirit of God's love, and you'll go a long way toward defusing it. However, some objects actually seem to deflect and defy such blessings. The *Ouija* board is one of them, which makes avoiding it even more important.

And for the record, I'm also not impressed with tarot cards, pendulums, palmistry, crystal balls, or other "props." Maybe it's just me, but they conjure up images of the kind of trickery that's been used to hurt and rob way too many people for hundreds and hundreds of years.

One of the challenges that few people are aware of during readings is how discerning you have to be when a client is experiencing unknown entities around them. Are these spirits who are alive and well on the Other Side? Are they earthbounds? Are they live people who are good at astral projecting to the point that they can actually appear in spirit form? Or—more rare than you might imagine—is your client suffering from a mental illness of some kind?

There's also increased energetic activity around a person who has a prepubescent or pubescent youth in close proximity. Nandor Fodor's *The Haunted Mind,* a fascinating book (which, frankly, my mother made me read), brilliantly describes how the unbridled hormonal energy of puberty can not only cause things to go "bump in the night," but can make them "snap, crackle, and pop" as well. I remember that when my brother, Paul, was about 12 or 13, shortly after he went to bed his shoes would fly around all over his bedroom and thud into the walls. Mom, with all her knowledge and extreme practicality, would go to his door and yell, "Paul, wake up and stop that!"

Paul never said, "Stop what?" I think that between her not making a big deal out of it and his trusting on a sub-conscious level that he was somehow causing the distur-bance, he made it stop without having meant to start it in the first place.

I think that too many people address children in the wrong way. Kids are very impressionable and psychical-ly sensitive by nature. When people make too big a deal about such incidents, youngsters can become afraid, and that fear can actually augment the undisciplined kinetic energy that they're experiencing.

Everyone can heal, since it's nothing more than a transfer of energy from one person to another, with God using you as a "vessel"—and it's as simple as the laying on of hands. My mother has written about cell memory, so I won't go into that in great detail here, but I will brag and say that she had this phenomenon by the tail 30 years ago, while science is just now saying, "Perhaps there's some merit in addressing the cells, because just maybe they *are* sentient and responsive to commands."

I believe that all of us are made up of cells that contain memories of past lives, and when focused and directed, the energy within them can be used like a laser beam to pierce the darkness of the unknown and unlock the key to everything from illness to future events. Who's to say that even though your chart was written and preordained by you, you didn't write it so that you'd be a catalyst for the new millennium, when all people recognize their potential to foresee events, heal, and become more spiritual?

I personally don't believe that there's a person who's ever lived or ever will live who hasn't had a psychic experience. They may have called it coincidence (which I don't believe in), a hunch, a premonition, intuition, or déjà vu, or have dismissed it as some fluke . . . wrong! The truth is that all those phenomena are really marvelous road signs, as opposed to "just your imagination." Frankly, I think that the word *imagination* should only be used to refer to an illness- or drug-induced hallucination, and—let's face it—those are pretty rare, and there are exceptions even then. Make no mistake, when people who are dying see their deceased family members and friends, it's *not* their "imagination" and it's *not* the medication. Those loved ones coming to greet them and welcome them Home are as real as we are.

Mom and I were once at the bedside of a terminally ill woman named Dorothy from our Novus Spiritus congregation. Her family was there, and Mom, as always, got right to the point: "Don't let her suffer. Start telling her about the Other Side and the loved ones who are waiting there for her."

All of a sudden, Dorothy sat up and said, "Oh, Ruth, I'm so glad you could make it!" A murmur went through the room, and the family explained to us that Ruth, another relative, was well and happy and living in Denver.

Mom turned to me and whispered, "So they think."

The next thing we knew, Dorothy lay back, holding out her arms, and said "Ruth" over and over again . . . and within minutes, she was gone.

The family thought it was a shame that Dorothy hadn't at least been able to see someone from the Other Side before she passed away, but my mother just ignored them and pointed at the silent phone. Within maybe 10 or 15 seconds, it started to ring.

One of Dorothy's sisters answered. Her face turned whiter and whiter as we heard her say, "No! You can't be serious! When?" When she finally got off the phone, she turned to the rest of her family and said in a halted voice, "Ruth died six hours ago."

So Dorothy had indeed seen Ruth on the Other Side. She'd been visible to Mom, too—I was only about 14 at the time, and all I'd seen was a filmy, condensed mass in the shape of a woman.

Spirit sightings can also be caused by astral projection—when individuals who are either asleep or wide awake slip out of their bodies and go to visit a loved one or a favorite place. I astrally project to England a lot, where I spent happy past lives with my mother. Mom rarely astrally projects, simply because she doesn't enjoy it, but when she does, she loves to go to Kenya—her home in at least one past life.

Mom and I have had frequent debates about astral projection: She thinks we should spend as much time as possible while we're here rooted inside our bodies, while I argue that there's nothing wrong with flying around visiting other places every once in a while. I feel that it proves that the soul really is independent of its earthly body, and that we all carry the sum total of who we are from one lifetime to the next.

I have to pity the poor uninitiated parents of the kinetic child. They must wonder if their kid is possessed, or if some evil entity is directing them. In the long run, when the child learns to harness and properly channel this energy, they can follow in the footsteps of such similar spirits as St. Francis, Padre Pio, and other great healers. There are lots of incredible people like these who work anonymous miracles without their names ever becoming known—let alone famous—and they're as important in the army of God as those who've been officially recognized.

CHAPTER 6

TRUE PSYCHIC
ABILITY

It's no wonder that there's so much skepticism toward this calling of Mom's and mine, and—believe it or not—she and I are just as skeptical. I've never forgotten the shock of watching a hidden-camera report on a "healer" who supposedly removed a tumor from a patient's body without ever making an incision. The "tumor" was analyzed and found to actually be chicken fat. That kind of thing enrages me. When people come to you for help, they're at their most vulnerable, and I don't know how charlatans live with themselves when they trick people who are genuinely in need.

Of course, the more you believe, the stronger your conviction gets, and it's also true that the more time you spend around honest, gifted people who are practicing the healing arts, the more their ability rubs off. Montel Williams credits my mother for his spiritual growth and his increased psychic ability. I'm completely discreet, and I would never divulge the details of anything that was said to me in private, but since the incident that I'm about to relay was openly discussed on national television, I feel comfortable talking about it.

Montel and his young son (whom we call "Little Man" or "Little Montel") were at a friend's house, where the family had a dog. Montel kept getting an uneasy feeling that it was going to bite the child, and he expressed his concern to a few people, including the dog's owner, but was assured that if there was ever a docile animal, it was this one. Besides, Little Montel wasn't anywhere near the dog, and it seemed completely uninterested in him. . . .

But—sure enough—about an hour later out of nowhere, the dog leapt up and bit the boy on the face, just missing his eye and hitting the tear duct. Once it was confirmed that Little Montel was going to be fine, his father took a lot of good-natured teasing about how all of Mom's "psychic stuff" must be rubbing off on him. (Mom says that in the 11 years that she and Montel have been friends, and especially since he's been diagnosed with MS, she can see his psychic ability rise like a comet every time they talk.)

It's easy to dismiss psychic ability as deductive or inductive logical reasoning until you really start analyzing it closely. Then you come to realize that there were really no clues at all, and no warnings—you just "knew because you knew." There's no other explanation. All people have the ability, but it's dismissed by many as a sign of craziness, just a cheap scheme to make money, or the work of the devil.

I've always wondered why people suspect that psychic gifts—which, like all others, are an endowment from

God—come from the devil, when they don't have that same suspicion about the work of Jonas Salk, Thomas Edison, or Alexander Graham Bell. Those great contributors to humankind were obviously here to help, as are legitimate psychics. Why would anyone think that the devil would be behind a "plot" to make the world a better place?

True psychics aren't just interested in telling their clients about the past, present, and future—we also warn, console, give advice, and refer people to the right doctor, nutritionist, psychologist, and so forth. We can be the filters of society . . . the bridge between sanity and insanity. And very often we make a difference just by giving our clients permission to *be* who they are. If a person is convinced that he saw a Native American in his backyard, does that mean that he's crazy and needs to be put on prescription drugs? Maybe. Or, perhaps he really did see a person from some past time. Time, after all, isn't just in the "now"—it has holes and warps in it, which allows energy imprints and spirits from other eras to come through and be seen.

It's interesting that sometimes the more afraid people are of spirits, the more easily they can see them, because fear enhances energy, and entities can use that heightened power to gain strength and become even more visible. Some reports have erroneously claimed that spirits can drain human energy. Don't believe it, because it's really people, living entities, who can drain you. I've gone on several haunting investigations, and I've never found spirits to be draining—in fact, they usually give me a sense of euphoria and well-being. And when I know that I've helped release some poor soul who was stuck and begging for attention and guidance, it provides me with a real feeling of satisfaction.

As for doing several readings in a row, I'm tired afterward, like anyone else after a long day's work, but since the information I give my clients doesn't come *from* me but rather *through* me (from God), there's no way that I can feel drained. My real responsibility is to simply open the door and keep my channel clear for whatever God has to say.

A lot of doctors and scientists have spent countless hours studying my mother. She's been taped both in and out of trance (when she vacates her body and allows her spirit guide Francine to come in), in addition to being light metered, videotaped, poked with needles, and having every detail of her physiology monitored—and even biofeedback shows a space when Mom exits and Francine comes in. On every test, it appears as if Mom has actually died while the transition is taking place: There's no brain activity, and everything stops. She's sometimes a little confused when she "comes back," similar to someone who's awakened quickly out of a sound sleep and needs a moment to get his or her bearings. However, Mom's actually full of energy after a trance. It's almost as if God allows Francine to leave a little added jolt of power behind. And it wasn't long ago that Montel experienced Francine for the first time with my mother in full trance, and he openly refers to it as the most awesome experience he's ever had.

If you start practicing some basic psychic exercises— for example, seeing what you can emotionally pick up from or about other people—and you find yourself getting exhausted, chances are that one of two things are happening: (1) You're trying too hard and forgetting to "let go and let God" do it; or (2) your ego is too tied up in the fear of being incorrect. As I myself have experienced many times, the person who swears that you're wrong today will probably realize sooner or later that you were actually quite right.

Here's an example that's an excellent illustration of this point. The other day, Mom, Angelia, and I were at a store called Gilmore's, a family favorite that sells beautiful flowers and Christmas decorations. I was standing out of the way, watching my mother and daughter "Ooh" and "Aah" over a display of reindeer that they couldn't live without. I was wondering how much this was going to cost me when an attractive, heavyset woman marched up to me and announced, "You're Chris Dufresne, aren't you? I have a bone to pick with you."

Here we go, I thought, suddenly wishing that I were psychic about my own life so that I would have known to wait in the car.

"About 15 years ago, you gave a reading to my mother-in-law, who wasn't well," she continued. "As the reading came to an end, you said, almost as a throwaway, 'Your daughter-in-law will always take care of you, but she has to watch her weight. The heavier she gets, the higher her blood pressure will go.' My mother-in-law said, 'You're mistaken, Chris—she's as thin as a rail, although she has had some blood-pressure problems.'"

Apparently, when the two of them listened to the tape together after the reading, they'd decided I was right about so many other things that a few "mistakes" were understandable. The woman then looked me squarely in the eye and said, "Six months later I ended up taking care of her until she died, and look at me! I can't lose weight no matter what I do!" She laughed and added, "And it's all your fault!"

I laughed, too, but I also reminded her, "No, ma'am, I'm just the reporter—God is the editor." I could see that her blood-sugar and carbohydrate counts were sky-high, which cause water retention, and I suggested that she see a nutritionist. "Your problem's not salt, but sugar," I told her. I also recommended one of our ministers who specializes in past-life cell-memory problems. Once the issue that's causing the weight gain is pinpointed and exposed—such as a need for protection or having been starved in a previous incarnation—the past-life difficulty will be released, and the current problem that it's causing will be solved.

That, by the way, is another ability that Mom and I both feel strongly about—to trace a phobia or chronic physical difficulty and free the client from it, once and for all. There's nothing that can liberate the soul more quickly than the truth. Past-life regressions are very powerful tools. Hypnosis opens the subconscious to all the memories it's holding, which the conscious mind doesn't have access to. Some people don't have the time or money to invest in such regressions, but it's still the psychic's responsibility to look backward in order to find the source of negativity, and then "unplug" it. As my mother has said, "Once you find the nail and pull it out, the foot can finally stop hurting."

Cell memory goes deeper and is more intensive as a healing tool, but that's more Mom's forte than mine. Just as I can readily see spirits and talk to them, I much prefer to do readings in the here-and-now . . . and the future.

The entire psychic side of our family, though, seems to share a passion for health issues, despite the fact that the closest any of us have come to a medical degree is my great-great-grandmother, Lena, who was a midwife in Germany, as well as a practicing psychic. I see this same interest developing in Angelia, who not only insists on tending us all when we're sick, but is also remarkably adept at pointing out the area of the body that's causing the illness.

Another thing we all share is a disinterest in the rituals that some (so-called) psychics go through when they undertake a reading. Out come the props: the tarot cards, the pendulums, the crystal balls . . . and before you know it, the "psychic" is spreading salt around himself and the client, burning sage, and murmuring incantations. Some of these people even fast for a few hours or a day ahead of time. By the time they've put on the raven wings, hung the beads in the doorway, and pulled out every trick in the book to create drama, I can't see how they're not too worn out to proceed with the reading itself!

Over the years I've often been asked, "What's the main goal of your research?"

My answer is, "To help people find their path," not only spiritually—which is my main objective—but also on a practical level, such as finding the right career, feeling better physically, sorting out their love life and family problems . . . basically, all of the factors that come into play in every one of our lives. I also believe in revealing the negatives I see in order to either help my clients avoid future disasters or be prepared for them, and therefore get through them more easily.

My mother embraces those goals as well, but her strongest focus is survival research, proving that the soul triumphs over this mortal coil called life. I don't work with the same survival and afterlife cases that she does, but I've conferred with her on many of them, and we both devote several hours a week to charity cases on every possible subject, including the afterlife.

Mom averages about eight benefits a year, and even those are geared toward our existence here and beyond and always ask, *Why?* She was a headliner for the first time at the Showboat Casino in Atlantic City, and she was a little nervous about how well that particular audience would receive her. That night, she called me the minute that she got offstage, delighted at the warmth and affection that everyone had showered her with, and also fascinated with the fact that even the "high rollers" in the room wanted to know if their loved ones made it safely to the Other Side, where Mr. or Ms. Right was, how their health was doing, and so on. I've traveled with Mom all over the world, and if there's one thing I've learned, it's that human beings are all bound together by the same worries and fears.

You might think that this makes me feel some defeat as a psychic, but the reverse is true. I find it comforting that everyone has what we call "desert periods" and times of aloneness, waiting, grief, and uncertainty; and yet that with a little help, prayer, advice, and trust in their first instincts, people will make it through to live and even "sing" another day. I'm asked many of the same questions by my clients over and over again, but I never get tired of it, because the details of the answers are different every single time, and that keeps the readings fascinating from my point of view.

Take, for example, two separate readings I did in the same week recently, where both clients wanted help with the men in their lives. Sandra, a petite blonde in her late 30s, told me she was involved with a slightly built, dark-haired man named Bill, whom she was feeling insecure about. She had reason to feel that way: He was cheating on her. Did I tell her? You bet. She gasped, not expecting brutal honesty, but I wasn't about to sit there like a parrot telling her what I knew she wanted to hear, when it simply wasn't the truth. And this way she could make an informed decision about whether or not she wanted to stay with him.

Debbie, on the other hand, had been with a husky, sandy-haired man named Greg for three years. Her problem with him had nothing to do with cheating—it was about the fact that he either couldn't or wouldn't commit. I told her that he would if she was willing to wait a year. This is a perfect example of a crossroads, or an option written into her chart. My bet was that Debbie would wait, but I could also see in her chart that she could head off down a completely different road, and I told her so. She responded, "If I take that different road, then what?"

The answer was, "Then you'll be alone for seven years." She asked if I thought that she should wait for Greg. I told her yes, she should—he's a good man, and they're very good for each other. Same kind of issue, with different people and varied answers . . . and on and on it goes.

I'm not sure if people realize that one of the toughest parts of my work is staying on schedule (the same goes for Mom). It's not a question of discipline, it's the fact that on any given day when we already have several readings scheduled back-to-back, we're likely to get four to six emergency calls that we simply can't ignore—everything from suicide threats to major health crises—and the next thing you know, we're hours behind schedule. We've had clients get really furious about the fact that we're running late, but I have to wonder if they'd be so aggravated if it were *their* emergencies that we'd taken time out to deal with.

If I ever had doubts about the validity of charts and a legitimate psychic's ability to read them, it would have to vanish, since my mother and I, conferring as often we do about certain clients' problems (without naming names), invariably come up with identical conclusions. One of my least favorite categories of readings to tackle, though, I'm sorry to say, is for Mom's friends. Don't get me wrong—I like her friends. It's just that after the reading, they'll always go to her and bring up some part of the reading they may not have liked, saying, "This is what Chris said. Do you agree with him?" She can't read for friends whom she's grown too close to because she loses her objectivity, so I understand their impulse to come to me instead—but it can get very awkward.

Several years ago, a friend of Mom's came to me about her future in the music business. I told her the truth (and the intervening years have proven me right): "You're wasting your time. Get out of it." This friend was furious with me and never stopped talking to my mother about how wrong I was. Mom was nice enough not to complain to me about it, but I know it put her in a tough situation. So at that point I made a vow to never put either of us in that position again. On very rare occasions, she does readings for my friends, but I know that she feels the same way that I do about it—she'd really rather not.

Come to think of it, a lot of people working on developing their own psychic ability get unnecessarily discouraged much too soon by the difficulty they encounter reading for friends and loved ones—the most natural people for them to start practicing on. When you're emotionally involved, you're bound to let your own hopes, fears, and opinions about your loved one seep into what you see for them, and keeping yourself out the way is the first step to an accurate reading. If you're trying to unearth and/or re-fine your psychic gifts, then whenever possible, start with people who aren't familiar to you. They're the real test, and the likeliest candidates for your objectivity. If you read them well, you can count on them to tell their friends—not yours—and that's how you build a practice.

After you've begun reading for strangers, then by all means set limits to prevent them from becoming dependent on you. Reliance on even the most talented reader is unhealthy for the client, and it keeps the psychic from branching out and reaching other people who need help just as much. There are a handful of psychics out there whose egos demand that they be constantly surrounded by groupies and sycophants who tell them how wonderful and brilliant and gifted they are, and I find that appalling. The minute the ego gets involved, the psychic gift runs the risk of being contaminated, and that's something both Mom and I make it a priority to guard against at all times.

Life is full of obstacles—that's a given. We psychics aren't superhuman, and we're not here to knock down every one of those obstacles for our clients. We're just here to offer them the poles that can help them vault over as many hurdles as possible.

CHAPTER 7

CAREER COUNSELING

I've talked about taking the first steps in trying to develop your abilities, but I'm warning you now to skip the props and trappings—the flickering candles, piano wires, *Ouija* boards, and what have you. Rely on yourself . . . *you* be the channel through which God's information flows.

My mother still talks about being with some psychics who'd gathered to give a lecture. To satisfy one ritual-loving person in the group, they all had to eat a large chocolate bar and burn sage before they spoke. By the time she stepped up to the podium, Mom felt so sick to her stomach that she could barely concentrate on what she was saying. As she's commented (and I agree), "It's whatever floats your boat"—but why all the machinations if you know that God is with you, and your only motive is to let Him speak through you?

Every time I think I've heard it all in my 18 years of reading, someone's right there to prove me wrong (as if it's not enough that Mom is always reminding me to "never say never"). The other day I was on the phone with a client named Leticia, who suddenly said, "Wait a minute, Chris, I want to put someone on the phone."

There was silence, then more silence. I used the quiet to quickly scan her chart to see if I could figure out who it was she'd rushed off to retrieve, but all I could see was a German shepherd. Finally, she came back on the phone and asked, "Well, what do you think?"

"It's a beautiful dog, ma'am," I answered.

"I know that, but what can you tell me about her?" she replied, somewhat impatiently. (Notice she wasn't remotely impressed that I knew she'd put a dog on the phone!) I calmly explained that dogs don't have charts like we do, but I was sure that hers was happy. That seemed to satisfy her, and we were able to move on to another subject.

Several years ago, Mom and I were walking through a mall where a "psychic fair" was going on. We never participate in those things—I have no prejudice against them, but Mom has a problem with the word *fair* and the clients being out in the open, exposed, with no discretion or privacy. (She thinks that it looks unprofessional, and while it doesn't bother me, I do see her point.) At any rate, we were heading through a maze of tarot-card readers when we heard a supposed "psychic" announce to her client that the woman was cursed and should go straight to the bank and bring her back $4,000 in small bills.

Witnessing this, my mother, like an avenging angel, turned and verbally laid into the "psychic," calling her every well-deserved name in the book. Then she turned to the client and said, "This woman is a fraud! If you want to report her to the authorities, I'll be glad to help you." The "psychic" literally ran away, but unfortunately, the poor client was so unnerved by the whole thing that she escaped as quickly as possible, too. . . . Afterward, Mom and I headed back to our car and never went to a "psychic fair" again.

I'm sure that there are some well-meaning, legitimate psychics at those events who are just trying to get their careers started. But picture a doctor standing in the alley behind a hospital or clinic with a scalpel or a bottle of pills, offering medical help at a bargain price. That might sound like an extreme comparison, but if we psychics don't make sure to maintain our professionalism and act on our honesty and integrity in this business—which is already subject to an enormous amount of skepticism—how are we ever going to be respected for our genuine efforts to help society?

So how do I think a psychic should go about establishing respectability? Here are my suggestions:

- Rent and set up a clean, neat, professional office space.

- Obtain all the legitimate business licenses available, and become familiar with the Better Business Bureau.

- Form a valid, tax-paying corporation and become active in helping your community (proving that you can and want to be an asset, not a liability or embarrassment).

- Never, ever even imply that you consider yourself to be an alternative to medical/psychiatric help.

Above all, remember that you are a spiritual counselor—nothing more and nothing less—and subject to the same laws, taxes, standards, and practices by which any valid business operates. And if you're interested in expanding into the hypnosis area, don't even consider it until you're legitimately certified, which takes 120 hours of study in "fielding service" (pro bono work with a certified hypnotist in attendance).

The career itself is not a learned process—it's a job. You can certainly uncover a buried psychic talent within yourself, but even then, you'll need more than just precognitive accuracy: It's a day in, day out responsibility, dealing with one person after another after another, with no rolling of the eyes or gritting of the teeth. When everything flows right, it's like a powerful, sparkling river—and it's an amazing, privileged joy.

Be prepared, though, for the fact that even the most well-meaning people can't seem to resist asking you questions. A nice, quiet evening can become very draining when you've made dinner plans with a couple, only to find six or eight people waiting for you at the restaurant because that couple mentioned that they were having dinner with a psychic to friends, who then begged to come along. At that point, the conversation goes like this: "I don't want to bother you . . . but could I just ask you a few questions?"

You're trapped, and—especially if you're a do-gooder—saying no is not an option, and those "few" questions can end up monopolizing the whole evening. I don't really blame people, but sometimes I feel like a dentist who's asked by guests at a cocktail party if he'd be willing to take a quick look at their molars. If my mother and I were paranoid, we could easily start to wonder if people like us for ourselves, or only for our abilities. Thank God we have such a strong base in our family, and our staff and ministers (who've been with us forever) realize how hard we work and respect the fact that our downtime is our downtime.

Come to think of it . . . sometimes they actually respect that fact a little *too* much. Occasionally, Mom or I will tell a staff member or minister something we've detected with our abilities, and they'll just go merrily on their way, as if we were merely oddballs whom they'd bumped into on the street. More than once I've heard my mother practically scream, "*Hello!* I'm speaking psychically now—you might want to listen!"

Ten years ago Mom told one of our secretaries to get dentures. The woman nodded politely but did nothing about it. . . . Fast-forward through ten years of agonizing oral surgery, root canals, bone disease, abscesses, antibiotics, and teeth actually crumbling right out of her mouth, and she's just now finally gotten around to buying dentures! The other day I heard her say, "I wish that I'd listened to Sylvia." I couldn't help but think, *Yeah, I guess you do!* But as Mom often says on this subject, "A prophet in their own land is always a stranger."

Lindsay Harrison, my mother's co-author on several of her books, called the office one day to check on the dosage of some herbs that Mom had recommended for her. Lindsay knows the staff very well, and after she left the message, she couldn't resist adding, "You see, unlike *some* people I could name, when Sylvia tells me to do something, I drop everything and run to get it done!" The staff members still chuckle about that, since they can't figure out for the life of them why they so casually ignore advice from someone whom other people travel halfway around the world to see!

It's been my experience that most psychics (my mother definitely *not* included) prefer to stay in the background, and believe it or not, the most difficult part of the profession for me is public appearances—either doing lectures or being on television.

People have said, "But Chris, if you stay too private, how are people supposed to know what you can do?" My answer is: "By doing numerous readings year after year." While I may not be reaching as many people as I would on TV, I'm still getting the benefit of word of mouth—which I'm grateful to say is very good. My mom and I agree that if you were to drop us anywhere and give us four or five people to start with, we'd still be able to build a hefty clientele.

As much as Mom enjoys the spotlight, she also considers it a necessity. It's her mission to balance her psychic message with her spiritual one. I can't emphasize enough that as common as psychics are these days, the qualities that she demands—such as morality, ethics, truth, and conscience—are rare.

If you're thinking about becoming a psychic, but you're more interested in your own ego than in the higher good—or if you're considering doing it for fame or wealth, instead of out of a genuine concern for humanity—then you must stop right now.

In life there's always a flip side to every coin. If I had any of this to do over, would I even think of changing it? Of course not. This is my God-given, chosen field from now until the end of this lifetime. Hard? Yes. Exasperating? Definitely. Fulfilling? Absolutely! You see, when it's good, it's *so* good that there's no other high like it.

Earlier in my career, I was trained to do hypnosis—but unlike my mother, it's not my forte. I will say this, though: The experiences that I've had with it have been close to miraculous. Taking a person back to a past time to release a chronic pain or phobia is a jaw-dropping thing to witness.

Out of the few hundred hypnosis sessions that I've done, one stands out. My client on this occasion was a woman named Julia who wanted very much to lose weight but just couldn't seem to accomplish it. It was fascinating and startling to see how, through hypnosis, she quickly connected to the problem. You see, around A.D. 800, Julia was kicked out of her house by her husband, who accused her of being unfaithful. She wandered around the desert for years after that, alone and literally starving to death. In her current life, she was recalling that hunger and simply couldn't get enough to eat. Even when she ran errands or took short car trips, she brought food with her for fear that she'd run out. Once she faced her past-life trauma, Julia was able to release it, and her relationship with food became relaxed and normal.

You really can't fool the mind when it comes to the truth—it'll latch on to it every time. As my mother says, "If you find the thorn or help the client find it and then pull it out, the problem's gone." I saw Julia about eight months later and could hardly recognize her—she was 87 pounds thinner!

Many of our ministers travel with Mom and set up hypnosis regressions and study groups all over the country. One of the reasons that our business works when other parapsychological institutes fold is that we stay active with our psychics, healers, hypnotherapists, and teachers. Many of those other organizations get so involved in research that they forget to focus on the individual. Statistics on what works and what doesn't are meaningless without face-to-face experience doing readings, noticing trends, making referrals, and having successes and even failures.

My mother also goes out on haunting investigations, which sound a lot spookier than they actually are. At the Winchester Mystery House, Mom picked up on an earth-bound maid and gardener, and I went with her on the Moss Beach Distillery haunting investigation that she did for *Unsolved Mysteries*. Not only did I have the pleasure of seeing her in action then, but—I'm also proud to say—I saw and heard everything that she did, and even put my three cents in as well. The most exciting thing about hauntings to Mom and me is the absolute proof they provide that the soul survives death—whether it makes it through the tunnel right away or stays behind awhile.

Ghosts are easier to see than spirits because they haven't fully transcended this plane and arrived on the Other Side yet. I know that people get discouraged when they can't see their deceased loved ones in living color, but what they often don't realize is that if those loved ones are too present, visible, or audible, then it means they haven't made it through the tunnel. We psychics can get in touch with both spirits and ghosts, of course, but when we run into ghosts, it's our moral responsibility to urge them to find the light and go to God—we can't leave them trapped between heaven and hell (heaven being the Other Side and hell being right here on Earth).

Even if you can't see spirits around you, you can watch for the hundreds of signals they use to let you know that they're around: a picture falling, a clock stopping for no reasons, lights blinking, clicking noises, or the inexplicable scent of flowers.

CHAPTER 8

THE PSYCHIC "MUSCLE"

While Mom and I take voluminous notes on the find- ings, trends, and conclusions that our clients reveal to us, the only tapes made of the sessions go to the clients themselves. We consider our oath of confidentiality to be sacred, even when it only involves protecting the identi- ties of our clients. If a person calls the office to ask if her husband is there getting a reading, our staff won't divulge that information. And believe me, people can get very ner- vous about the whereabouts of their spouses.

One of our ministers once asked Mom why her hus- band had left her. My mother put her arms around her to cushion the blow as best she could, and answered: "Be- cause there's another woman." She then described his mis- tress right down to the last detail. The next day the min- ister told Mom that she'd passed this information along to her husband. After a long silence, he'd replied, "God, Sylvia's good."

My mother constantly says, "If you really don't want to know, don't ask," and I always agree.

And speaking of what *not* to do, I beg you not to fall for a scam that I keep hearing about. It goes like this: Someone says, "For a fee, I can make your wayward lover fall back in love with you." Believe me—that's simply not possible. In fact, it's as ludicrous as a psychic's claim that for a generous advance payment, he can give you next week's lotto numbers.

When people receive insights, they sometimes ask how they can differentiate between a psychic impulse and their imagination. The best way that I've heard of comes from my mother: "Get rid of that damnable word 'imagination.'" Look it up: *Imagination* simply means "imagery, from images known." This seems informative until you start examining that definition more closely. Let's say, for example, that you "imagine" a wang doodle. How is that possible, according to the definition, if you have no idea what a wang doodle is? From now on, try to get into the habit of assuming that you're getting a psychic impulse *first*—as opposed to just imagining things—and see how many fascinating possibilities open up to you.

Although a lot of people also try to dismiss their past-life memories as something that they're just imagining, it's worth pointing out that after one of our ministers does a regression on someone, more often than not Mom and I will separately pick up on exactly the same past lives that the minister just uncovered. The odds against us being able to independently guess that information are staggering, and we're *definitely* not mind readers.

Psychic ability can start at any point in life. Obviously, in my family—as in other ones—some of us are born with it. But many individuals report that they experienced precognitive events when they were younger but shut them out, fearing that they'd somehow be regarded as weird. Then they find that these occurences return later to the point that it's simply impossible for the people to ignore them.

Traumatic events and serious illnesses can augment psychic ability, too—as can highly intense emotions. Mom has said that she's always "on" psychically . . . but make her mad and her already-amazing gift positively soars. That's why I'm convinced that the ability resides in the emotional side of the brain, and that—without meaning to sound sexist—mediums are more often women than men.

I'll always say that the hardest part of developing psychic ability is learning to notice and trust your first impression. Either this difficulty occurs because the ego becomes involved and doesn't want to be wrong, or because you think that anything that comes too easily can't be true. For all our talk about initial impressions and our ability to accept them on our clients' behalf, Mom and I still don't always pay attention to them ourselves. After we've second-guessed our feelings and ended up in trouble, we always want to kick ourselves down the street. We remind each other a lot that everything is a learning experience.

We also often comment that if we had to think up what to say during readings, it most likely wouldn't be what actually comes through. Psychic information works beside and through you, but never *from* you. The more you practice it, the more the psychic "muscle" gets stronger and the more reliable it can become.

Psychic phenomena are not new to what some people foolishly refer to as "primitive" societies. Mom hates that word, because when she traveled to Kenya, and even deep into the bush, the natives recognized her gift. In fact, an old wise woman of the Samboro tribe refused to read for her, saying, "Why ask me? You do the same thing that I do." Similarly, an Egyptian woman from a small village once told my mother, "You have *sight!*" Mom asked how she knew, and the woman replied, "You have a light around you."

This reminds me of the first time that Mom met Lindsay Harrison's housekeeper, Maria. Maria works five days a week and doesn't watch television, so she'd never seen Mom before, and while she speaks English very well, the only reading she does is in her native Spanish. Although she knew that my mother and Lindsay write books together, she had no clue what those books were about. After they were introduced, the minute Mom left the room, Maria ran over excitedly, gestured toward her eyes and face, and—as if it were going to be news to Lindsay—whispered: "Your friend is psychic [pronouncing it 'SEEK-ick']! Very seek-ick!"

Lindsay just smiled and said, "No kidding."

CHAPTER 9

CHALLENGES AND WORDS OF ADVICE

The biggest challenge that my mother and I face right now is trying to catch up on our backlog of readings. Going on the road so much these days, Mom loses a lot of income. It's a catch-22 in a way: She needs to go out and lecture because she adores reaching thousands of people at one time with her spiritual teachings (which is part of what makes her so unique), but when she's on the road, she feels guilty about not being able to do readings.

I keep telling Mom to let herself off the hook, and she just smiles and assures me that at age 69, she thinks that things are already pretty great. Besides, as she's well aware, there's a history of longevity in our family—one great-uncle, Henry, kept working until he was 96! So, despite the amazing nonstop schedule that she keeps up, my mother has good reason to believe that she's got a lot of time left to accomplish any number of incredible things.

Novus Spiritus, the beating heart of our organization and its spiritual core, has now released its 30 years of research in a set of books entitled the *Journey of the Soul* series, through the company that is publishing this book, Hay House. The information in these books was gathered from trance sessions with my mother's guides, Francine and Raheim, reporting on all the records and resources available to them on the Other Side. This is fascinating reading for one simple, irrefutable reason: Nothing resonates in the soul like the truth. When it hears it, the soul almost cries out: "I remember this like a familiar, cherished memory. I know this is right."

Since when we're at Home, we know the truth, it really *is* something that we remember—which makes us treasure it even more. I often wonder how much better this world would be if we could just cut through all the manufactured complications of life and return to the basics—the simple truths that Christ taught. As the gospel of St. Thomas quotes Jesus in the Dead Sea Scrolls: "I am everywhere, under a rock or a stick, and I will always be there."

As I write this, Mom and the staff are preparing for another road trip. The back room of the office is filled with flyers, products, books, tapes, pins, and other items, which Darren is boxing up. Michael is taking inventory; Tom is checking the audio equipment; Linda is running around, picking up last-minute travel items; Mary is wading through a huge pile of mail; and Pam is trying to field calls with Vera and Helen.

Mom's going to be filming six *Montel* shows and has a meeting with one of her publishers, so she has a million things on her mind—but she still finds time to call me and ask if her beloved grandson Willy is getting better from his cold. I talk to her about a sensitive topic that one of the prime-time investigative shows wants to discuss with her, although she doesn't want it to be publicized. She'll be appearing on *Larry King*, speaking in Indianapolis, and then heading to St. Louis for a children's benefit. The staff members have to make sure that she has everything she needs for this amazing variety of activities—and they handle it all seamlessly, knowing that they'll also be doing follow-ups on our study groups and the many people who'll be signing up for regressive-hypnosis sessions.

Mom tells me that she wants me to do a live chat session on **MSN.com**, and also agrees to arrange for me to be on the Kelly & Kline radio show. I know that even though I'm not wild about the limelight, I'd better work myself up to it or I'm going to look downright lazy compared to her!

My children arrive, and my daughter immediately starts helping with the task of labeling, while my son settles in to play with the dogs. The whole thing reminds me of a zoo, full of the world's happiest animals. Five of the ministers are there as well—they travel to Mom's speaking engagements on a rotation system, with two or three of them always in attendance, depending on the size of the crowd. I'll be going to the Los Angeles, San Diego, and San Francisco lectures, not only because they'll all be huge, but also because they're close to home, and I won't lose much work time.

A client named Miriam arrives, and I escort her into my reading room. She's had a terrible tragedy: the death of her two-month-old baby from SIDS (sudden infant death syndrome). She's feeling an enormous amount of grief, but is spiritual enough to know that her infant is with God.

But understandably, the human part of her wants to know why this happened. I explain that there are a certain number of hours, days, months, and years that we choose to spend on this planet, and when that time's up, we graduate. We can use our time on Earth to learn, overcome negativity, and become stronger, or we can go around angrily hating God. In times of grief, we're allowed to feel that way as part of the process, until we come to be aware of the reality that life here is fleeting, and the tougher our lessons, the more we learn.

In my next reading, the client, whose name is Adrian, starts out by saying, "Well, I didn't want to come here, but my wife forced me." Most psychologists that I know would excuse a person like that, telling him to come back when it's *his* idea to be there—but I don't. Maybe it's because I want to prove what psychics can do, and some of my competitiveness comes into play. Anyway, I begin describing Adrian's deaf left ear, an abscess on his bottom right molar, and a throbbing pain in his ankle. It's obvious that I've struck a nerve, so to speak—I definitely have his attention. I then inform him that he's about to start a baking business, which finally elicits the inevitable "How did you know?"

The self-evident answer is, "I'm psychic," but I never mind people asking. They're not stupid—it's just their first reaction to being caught off guard. In this case, now that I've validated myself, Adrian starts mellowing out, joking and asking questions, and we have a good time for the rest of the reading.

The hardest part of a reading is trusting the information that God gives you, even when you're confronted with a resounding "No!" from the client. It used to make me a little queasy, but I've since learned to forge ahead, remembering that if I didn't know things that my clients don't, they'd have no reason to be sitting in my office. How many of us would believe it if we'd been told ahead of time about all those life-changing moments: the illnesses, deaths, marriages, or great jobs that would transform us forever—seemingly in the blink of an eye?

It's funny, but most people call because they want to hear what's waiting for them in the future. Yet some of them will argue with me if I don't tell them exactly what they want to hear or what they've already decided I'm going to say. (How many times have any one of us said, "I'd never do that . . ." only to realize later that that's exactly what we ended up doing?)

The next client of the day, Hannah, has a medical problem. She's been everywhere trying to deal with it, and every doctor that she's seen has been stumped. I can see immediately that it's an adrenal-gland problem, and I refer her to an excellent endocrinologist. (I've subsequently found out that Hannah's problem was with both her adrenal gland and her pancreas, so I have to wonder why didn't I pick up on the pancreas, too. I believe that God gave me just enough information to get her to a specialist who'd check her out and take care of everything that was troubling her. What's important is that she regained her health—and in the end, I'm more concerned about that than I am about being just exactly right.)

The next person to come in is a man named Neil who believes that his phones are tapped, his TV is wired to monitor him, and the government is out to get him. There's no charge for this client—he was referred to us by a psychiatrist colleague of ours. Neil is angry when I assure him that those frightening beliefs aren't real, but he promises to see another colleague whom I know can help him. I know that most likely he won't, the poor guy. He'll probably find someone who'll milk his paranoia by telling him that he's been struck with a curse, which only that person can cure for X amount of money—in small bills, of course.

After Neil leaves, I could let myself get worried sick about him, but I've learned to release those concerns to God. I remember that I can only do as much as I can with truth and reason and must leave the rest up to the person himself. Feeling compassion is both what gets to me most and also what keeps me sane. I believe that if we lose this emotion, we'll never be balanced—we'll become hardened and uncaring, and ultimately ineffectual.

One thing that used to really haunt me was the question of what on earth I'd do if a really dark entity showed up in my reading room. I finally asked Mom about it and found out that it used to worry her, too, until she realized that such an entity would never come to a reading. These beings feel completely justified in their evil and are on a track all their own. Only good people worry about whether or not they're on the *right* track, and feel guilt, question their motives, or try to keep in step with their chart. If they think that someone can help them sort such things out, they're not too self-righteous to ask. And the ministers, priests, psychologists, friends—and yes, even psychics—who do the helping are those who are willing to listen and advise.

I understand how confusing it can get when you try to learn how to be more psychic, but there are some exercises that can really help strengthen the psychic "muscle." I can't stress enough that the most important step is always noting and trusting your first impression—no matter how ridiculous it seems—and the vibrations that you pick up, which apply to people, places, *and* things. My mother, for example, loves antiques, but she always touches them to detect their vibrations and the story behind the items.

Psychometry is the psychic art of being able to sense a person or object's past. That antique ring, piece of furniture, or figurine that you own still carries vibrations from everywhere that it's been before, including any serious illnesses its previous owners had, and depending on whether they were happy or sad, if their lives were peaceful or chaotic.

My mother says that there's nothing worse than telling a person a whole story about an object that she's asking about and having her reply, "I don't know. I just got it yesterday." When Mom was teaching about psychic phenomena at De Anza College, she did a demonstration of how psychometry works. She took a ring from a student and began to talk in great detail about a horseshoe-shaped bar in the late 1800s where a red-haired man walked in and was immediately shot by a young gunslinger.

The student just stared at Mom, shrugged, and said, "Beats me what that means. My aunt gave the ring to me a week ago."

Months after the class ended, the woman wrote to share what she'd learned about the ring since my mom's demonstration. It had originally belonged to the woman's great-grandfather but had been cut down to make a lady's ring. Her great-grandfather had indeed run a horseshoe-shaped bar, and the man who was killed was his brother.

I asked Mom if she minded not being publicly validated, and she replied, "Absolutely not." I feel exactly the same way: I don't obsess about being proven right, and I don't believe any budding psychic should either. One way or another the truth will reveal itself in the future. If you just keep reminding yourself that you're only the vehicle, the reporter, you'll drown out the false ego that's hanging you up.

I would also caution all beginning psychics to pay close attention to how they handle their own lives. I'm by no means judgmental, but I do know that any form of substance abuse can destroy the body and brain cells. I have a real aversion to drugs—I even had my wisdom teeth taken out with no anesthetic of any kind. Am I crazy? Maybe, but my mother is the same way. We're just not an addictive family—which is somewhat unusual, since many psychics and mediums have chronic substance problems, mostly with alcohol. My mom can't tolerate even one drop of alcohol. In fact, after a single sip she's been known to throw up. She and I both thank God for that particular aversion, because with the work we do, it would be easy to fall into the trap of trying to dull our minds against the pain we're exposed to.

Am I talking about prescription drugs that a doctor deems necessary for your health and well-being? Of course not—I'm talking about illegal substances or anything taken to an extreme that interferes with your good judgment or ability to think clearly. If Carlos Castaneda needed mushrooms to "see," that's not for me to criticize. But *I'll* always believe in doing it on your own. The "organic" spiritual high that comes from being psychic is like no other that you'll ever find.

Now this may sound almost like a contradiction, but here's another warning while you're developing your psychic abilities: Don't concentrate! Concentrating means that you're employing *your* intellect, when it's a far greater one than yours that you want to listen to. Once *that* intellect's information has come through you, your own can help by offering advice—but that's of secondary importance to what you're given. Besides, let's face it: It's not your chart you're trying to read, and not your destiny that you're being shown, so what business is it of yours, really, to try to make sense of it?

I'm also a big believer that the mind and the psychic gift can't flourish without a healthy body to house them. I work out four times a week, and I confess that I don't enjoy it. In fact, most of the time I hate it—but I hate that "dead weight" of not working out even more. And diet is incredibly important, too. I find it fascinating that 38 years ago a doctor told my mother that psychics are prone to low blood sugar. His theory was that this was due to the fact that the middle chakras, or energy centers, take such an emotional beating in psychics.

This makes sense when you think about it. . . . When you experience an emotional trauma, don't you feel as if you've been punched in the stomach? And when you have a strong instinct about something, don't you tend to describe it as a "gut-level" feeling?

A good preventive measure against low blood sugar is the high-protein diet that I've been enjoying for years. (Consult your doctor, though, before you undertake any dramatic change in diet.) I don't eat red meat, but I do eat chicken, turkey, and fish. My mother eats all kinds of meat—even (ugh!) liver, but I can't stand it. To compensate, I take supplements of complex amino acids and a lot of antioxidants. In addition, Mom, Montel, and I all go to the same doctors at the Palm Springs Life Extension Institute, and I've noticed the benefits even more for her than for myself. I'm 39, and Mom's 69, and her endurance through a schedule that would send most people to bed for a month never ceases to amaze me.

You don't have to be psychic to know that obesity is at an all-time high in the U.S., and I think that a major reason can be traced straight back to sugar. But that leads me to another observation: How many very thin psychics have you ever seen? Few, if any, right? I'm convinced that extremely sensitive people have a greater tendency to sub-consciously put on weight as a means of protecting them-selves—with the factor of past-life cell memory contribut-ing as well.

And while you're making your physical and emotion-al health a major part of your daily life, above all, *never* neglect your spiritual well-being or forget one simple yet critical truth: Without God, you are nothing.

CHAPTER 10

PSYCHIC EXERCISES

The exercises for developing your psychic "muscle" start off pretty simply, but I guarantee that they're important for sensitizing your third eye—your sixth sense—and giving you the confidence that you'll need. This chapter includes a few exercises to get you going.

Have a friend gather several pieces of colored construction paper while you blindfold yourself. Then, ask her to hand you one piece of paper at a time, and try to sense what color it is. Ask yourself as you hold it if it feels cool (green or blue) or warm (orange, red, or yellow). With practice, you'll be surprised by how accurate you become at identifying the color of the paper without ever looking at it.

After you try that, you can have someone put an object in an empty coffee can and replace the lid. (Start with something simple like an egg.) Hold the can, and try to sense what the object is. Is it plain or colored? What shape do you feel that it is? Keep asking yourself similar questions, noting your first impressions, and then start narrowing down the possibilities. Again, with increased practice, you'll be amazed at how close you can come to guessing right.

For another good exercise, have your friend or partner cut out pictures from a magazine, put them in separate envelopes, and then "guess" what the object in each picture is. (Again, keep the images simple.) Is it a person, place, or thing? What shape and color is it? Keep practicing until your instincts come to you more and more quickly—with increased ease will also come better accuracy.

These exercises won't initially help you predict the future, obviously. But they will assist you in becoming comfortable with the experience of "seeing" the unseen, and this will guide you right past the finite reality that we're taught to accept as "all there is."

The next two exercises are more complicated and should only follow after you've done a lot of work with the previous ones:

1. Ask a practice partner in a different location to stop whatever he's doing at a mutually agreed upon time, and then concentrate on the details of his surroundings. At the appointed time, have a blank piece of paper and a pencil in hand, and begin to describe or draw wherever it is you "see" your partner. Is there a building? Water? A tiled floor? Does your partner "feel" inside or outside? Is it warm or

cool? Is he standing or sitting? If he's sitting, does what he's sitting on feel soft or hard? The more questions that you ask yourself, the more precise you'll learn to be and the better you'll get at this phenomenon—which is called "remote viewing."

2. Try "automatic writing." Sit down at a desk or table, and rest your arm comfortably so that your writing hand and the pen it's holding are in a relaxed position above a blank piece of paper. (I have no idea why, but for some reason this exercise always works best for me with a ballpoint pen.) Then, without letting your own mind or will interfere in any way, let the pen start gliding on the paper on its own. At first it may just make circles or scribbles, but—if you keep at it several times a week for a few weeks—sooner or later it's very probable that actual words will begin to form. Don't get discouraged, however, no matter what happens—just keep going and don't force it. When you become adept at this exercise, you'll find that it's much more accurate than *Ouija* boards, which carry negative vibrations, as I've said before. And when you start to get messages, wait to see whether they're real or just subconscious wishes . . . with practice, you'll be able to tell the difference.

What you'll find overall is that the more you practice, the more psychic information will pour in at exactly the right time (even when you're not doing the exercises themselves).

For example, take a situation where you're talking to someone who's grieving. All of us can get tongue-tied at first when we're faced with a soul in real torment. But with the help of the exercises I've just described, exactly the right thoughts and words can pour out of your mouth. How many times have you thought that you didn't know what to say, but suddenly you started talking and what you said actually helped, and you later thought, *I don't know where that came from*? This is what that often-misinterpreted word *channeling* really means. When something's coming from God and not you, it rolls right off your tongue and gives much comfort and peace.

Sensitive people in highly emotional situations have been known to lapse into trancelike states, speak in foreign tongues, see visions, and so forth. Mom's research shows—and the doctors whom she's worked with have concluded—that these things come from the "limbic" or "primitive" part of the brain. This part of the brain acts like a vessel, ready to receive precious words of truth, as long as we remove the "stoppers" of stress, ego, and will—three things that have to be sacrificed in order for it to work.

In readings, it really is just God, you, and the client. You have to be ready and pray that your "vessel be cleared," and that you engage your intellect and emotion to form a complete balance. And whatever comes through—however outrageous or silly or depressing it may seem—your integrity and commitment to God demand that you say it.

CHAPTER 11

EMOTIONAL
READINGS

I've just finished my readings for the day. I take a break, make a bathroom stop, drink a cup of tea, and go back to sort through some mail again. It piles up, but my mother and I always read our mail. I look at the clock and am relieved to see that I'm right on time.

Mom's door is closed—a signal that she's involved in a phone reading. We've installed a phone system that no one can tap or break in to, so we can guarantee absolute privacy. When Linda sees the light on my mother's private line go off, she informs me: "She's off now, if you want to talk to her."

I open Mom's door, and she's sitting with her head in her hands. I know the posture—I've been there. "A rough one?" I ask.

She nods. "A five-year-old who drowned."

"Are you okay?"

"Sure, honey," she says. But there's always empathy: What if that child had been one of ours?

No matter how psychic you are, you can't completely separate yourself from other people's grief. Like Mom, if I ever become immune to the heartbreak of my clients, I'll quit. Spirituality saves us from being pessimists, but we're still human. Did that five-year-old make it safely to the Other Side? Yes, of course, but that doesn't spare the parents from feeling so much grief and loss.

I close the door to give Mom some private time to regroup, but before I go back into my own room, I see her light go back on and know that, like me, she's been able to shake off her emotions and has moved on to the next client. It's hard to explain, but readings like that go into a mental box, to either take out and look at later, or to send "express" to God. For the time being, the next reading is a new adventure, bad or good—a different life, a fresh chart to read—and our success rides on the accuracy of what lies ahead.

During any emotional reading, it's almost like a switch that turns on or off in your brain. There's sadness or joy, then a rush, and finally that curtain closes and another opens. It's almost like seeing several different plays in the same evening—each one can bring out a different emotion. You may laugh and weep your way through one, but then that play ends and the next begins, and you're completely engrossed again with the new cast and story or—in the case of my mother and me—the new client and chart. Mom has reminded me that movie theaters used to show double or even triple features, and none of them overlapped or interfered with each other. That's how it feels for us doing many readings on any given day.

It's fascinating how there seem to be themes among clients' questions that run in cycles. We'll get an entire day of people who are mourning a recent death, for example, or a steady stream of clients, all of whom want our help in locating a missing loved one. Mom recently did an **MSN.com** chat on the Internet, and the moderator actually commented about these patterns. During a previous chat that Mom had done, everyone had relationship questions; during the one after that, the prevalent subject was missing children; and another dealt almost exclusively with pets. And it's always the participants, not Mom, who control where the chat's going to go. Mom has no more control over it than she or I have over the clients—none of whom know each other—who come, one after another, to our reading rooms.

These recurring patterns among strangers have led us to conclude that people in pain seem to telepathically follow others with similar ailments, and that psychic forces work on many levels, on a far grander scale than any of us can possibly imagine.

CHAPTER 12

OUR ORGANIZATION, AND A FEW PSYCHIC METHODS

Obviously, a successful and legitimate psychic organization can't sustain itself without income from a
sound source—a working group of psychics, healers, and
spiritual counselors.

It took many years for the organization that my mom
founded to really establish itself. She started out in an office with two rooms and felt so closed in and claustropho-
bic that she hung curtains over a bare wall to create the
illusion that there was a window. And since telecommu-
nications were hardly what you'd call "sophisticated" in
those days, when Mom was doing a reading or a past-life
regression, my grandfather (who worked with her at the
time) had to take the phone off the hook for the duration
of the session.

In addition, in those days, my mother lectured every
Tuesday night at the Congregational Church. Looking

back, my only conscious memory of those lectures was that I never attended them without a big bag of beef jerky—but I also know that I listened and absorbed a whole lot more than I realized at the time.

From that tiny office, we moved to a larger place with a staff, but Mom was still the only source of income. She taught four nights a week, and my brother and I would sit in the back of the class and do our homework. She also did private trances in people's homes, and I remember her saying that sometimes she felt like the most unique barbecue party in town. People came to listen to her, test her, and to taunt her, and to this day I marvel at the courage that it must have taken, how unnerving it must have been, and how confident my mother had to be in her gifts to keep on going. She organized spaghetti dinners, garage sales, craft fairs, rummage sales—you name it—until we finally realized that these things were costing more to put on than we were making from them!

But again, little by little, if you're talented and legitimate, two people tell four people, those four tell ten, and your clientele grows and flourishes. In Mom's case, of course, she eventually started getting major boosts from her countless TV appearances, but even before that, she was booked for readings six months in advance and was constantly busy.

By the time I came on board 21 years ago, we had a staff of seven and room for more classes. Then the ministry started, and today we're blessed with 62 ministers and ministers-in-training—not including deacons and novitiates from study groups. Our employees number 20 now . . . and we're understaffed. Many have been with us in some capacity or other for at least 28 years, and between them and the ministers, we've become a family, seeing each other through deaths, births, illnesses, and a lot of shared joy.

The ministers teach classes and manage study groups composed of people from all over the country and the world, who gather to study and discuss our spiritual material for a minimal cost per month. A minister liaison studies what's going to be talked about—as well as a tape of Mom's lectures or sermons—and conducts the meetings. Today, the study groups number in the hundreds. We also put out a newsletter, published by Hay House, which gives my mother's timely philosophy on a variety of subjects and answers readers' questions, analyzes their dreams, and presents an astrological forecast. (I also contributed to the newsletter when Hay House included an excerpt from my first book.)

Before long, Mom and I will have 34 books on the market between the two of us, and we still do several readings a day. Why? Because with the mounting mail, phone calls, and e-mail, plus our online cyberministry, study groups, church services, classes, and lectures, the office isn't just buzzing—it screams! We've outgrown our office, but we can't even pretend that we're able to afford to move just yet. Come to think of it, the only complaint that I've ever heard from my mother is, "Why does payroll seem to come up every three days?!"

In other words, being a psychic and reading for people is glorious. But it's even more so knowing that this gift of ours is going toward a greater good—a theological society that provides countless services free of charge, gives people a safe place to come and be welcomed with open arms, and at the same time, provides so many individuals with a career that enables them to learn and make a living. I often look around in amazement at all the people and families we support . . . and damn, it's a great feeling!

One form of the psychic gift is telepathy, which means that you receive messages from a sender. It's really more common than you might think, and some people are so adept at it that a wife might be able to send a mental message to her husband to bring home a loaf of bread, for instance, and he'll stop at the store on his way home . . . sometimes without even realizing where the idea came from. Often the message seems random, like a TV transmission: You don't see it, but you receive it.

A good way to practice this particular ability is to team up with a friend and tell her, "At 9 P.M., I'll send you a message." At 9:00, both of you should find a quiet place, be still, and picture a blackboard with a message being written on it by you for the receiver to read. Keep the message simple at first—something like "I miss you." After a few attempts, the receiver might say that she couldn't see anything on the blackboard but did get a sense or feeling of longing, and that's close enough.

Symbols are also good things to practice transmitting. Try using the Rhine card deck or make one of your own containing a star, square, circle, squiggle lines, and so on. Sit holding one of the card symbols and try to transmit it to your receiver. These cards are very effective and have been used several times to prove conclusively that people really can send and receive thoughts. (How many times have *you* called someone on an "impulse," only to hear him say, "I've been thinking about you all day!"?)

Why doesn't the information always make it to its target? One reason is that some people are better at receiving and others are better at sending. If you and your friend try switching roles a few times, you'll discover very quickly the one that you're more comfortable with.

If you send and send and nothing happens, it could be that you don't know how to really let go of the message. If you carry a letter without ever sending it, it obviously never reaches its destination. Similarly, if you broadcast a message telepathically but let your mind get diverted too quickly, it'll never reach its target either. If the blackboard image isn't effective for you while you're practicing this skill, try using the visual image of mentally writing your message on a piece of paper, putting it in an envelope, sealing and stamping the envelope, addressing it to your chosen receiver, and dropping it in an express mailbox—one that says, "Mental delivery in 30 minutes." Then get busy with anything and everything else. Try this exercise for a week and you'll be amazed at the results.

ESP, or extrasensory perception, is very similar but far more simplified. It's the ability to detect energy, positive or negative, without necessarily putting a name to it. This is the reason that some people can walk into a place and immediately feel good, bad, or indifferent. It's close to psychometry, the ability to hold an object and sense its past vibrations, which I discussed earlier. Neither ESP nor psychometry is useful in predicting the future, but they're both helpful tools and very much worth developing.

One easy exercise to try is the pendulum. Suspend a crystal from a string, and hold the string between your thumb and forefinger. Balance your elbow on a table so that the crystal is an inch or two above it and can move freely. Now, begin asking questions about the present (not the future)—keeping them simple at first—and watch the movement of the crystal. It'll move from right to left to indicate *no,* toward and away from you for *yes,* and in a circle if the answer is *I don't know.* The pendulum can give you insights not only into what's happening in your life, but also into your own subconscious mind.

Tarot cards are another method of fortune-telling. I personally feel that if you have to use visual aids, you're not "taking" your first psychic impression, but if such objects help you get started, there's nothing wrong with them. The tarot is interesting, particularly the Rider-Waite deck because many historians believe it's where our playing cards come from. Frankly, though, I can't imagine sitting in front of a client and watching the devil or death card reveal itself. What would you say? In tarot, those cards can actually indicate new beginnings—but even so, you might have a lot of explaining to do.

Like my mother, I consider the *Ouija* board strictly off-limits. Far too many clients have come into our office who've been frightened unnecessarily because, without understanding what was happening, they accidentally made contact with a negative and opportunistic wandering spirit on the *Ouija* board. You don't throw your door open to any old stranger who happens to show up, so why subject yourself to the spiritual version of that by "playing" with a *Ouija* board?

Mom and I differ on the subject of automatic writing, however. I've never been a fan, but she feels that those people who do it are using their own energy with the help of a guide or higher consciousness. However, writing down what a spirit says seems very laborious to me. Again, if it helps you "tune in" at first, that's fine. But I'd rather see you spend your time just practicing asking yourself questions and letting God move through you.

Clairaudience is the ability to hear your spirit guide or the souls of people who've made the transition to the Other Side. Despite the clairaudient gifts of my mother and grandmother, I'm not a medium. My guide, Charlie, doesn't really communicate with me audibly—it's more like a series of thought processes that I can tell are quite distinct from my own. It takes some practice to know the difference, but it can start as simply as wondering, *Why would I have thought of that?* or *Why was I thinking of Susan all day?* Act on those thoughts and they get stronger. Of course, Mom has complete verbal contact with her spirit guide Francine, who even comes into her body to give information. It's only different from doing a psychic reading insofar as you're communicating with someone who has more "in-house" knowledge of God, creation, and our purpose here when you're talking directly to a guide. Francine will occasionally answer questions about her own life, but she's much more strongly rooted in the spiritual realm.

Palm reading is another practice used to divine the future. Palmists believe that there are specific lines on the hand that denote the length of life, marriages, children, accidents, and other major events, and that there's a mound beneath each finger that implies some knowledge of the past or future. I don't really have any objection to palm reading. I like the physical-contact aspect of it—touch can help to calm a nervous client . . . or an anxious amateur reader, for that matter.

It continues to fascinate me that Mom and I have been accused of not being "real" psychics because we don't use palmistry, tarot cards, or any other such tricks of the trade. People are certainly entitled to their own opinions. The bottom line with palmistry, as with all the other visual aids that I've been discussing here, is that if it helps you develop your skills, fine—but please don't let it interfere with your communication with God, Who is always your *real* source of information.

There are also those people who do readings via handwriting analysis, which is the study of the size, shape, slant, openness, and so forth of the letters in a client's writing. Some practitioners of handwriting analysis will offer nothing but a general reading that could apply to anyone. Others are more serious about it, and study handwriting for everything from determining employees' honesty to assisting in medical diagnoses. Learn about it if it interests you, of course . . . but only as a tool—not a replacement—for the psychic skills that you're trying to develop.

This leads me to astrology and numerology, both of which I believe have merit. My mother has studied these more extensively than I have, but we both feel that at the heart of all the math, signs, houses, trines, and planetary locations lies the ultimate truth of the direction on our life path—which only God can provide.

Crystal-ball and water-gazing (sometimes known as scrying), have been popular for centuries, and are not as far-fetched as they might sound. Think of the old crystal radio sets if you doubt that crystals can transmit energy . . . and we all know that water is a great energy conductor—that's why spirit and ghost activity is more prominent in the very early-morning hours, when the dew is at its heaviest.

Regardless of which of these vehicles you use (if any), be sure to start every reading by surrounding yourself with the white light of the Holy Spirit. As I've said before, this accomplishes two things: (1) It's a way of asking God to help you only receive valid information, and (2) it protects you from any negative energy that might try to take advantage of your openness.

So with the available alternatives in mind—sitting around a table holding hands, conducting a séance, casting bones or stones, or reading palms or handwriting—never, ever forget that it's always best to take advantage of your own "receiving vessel" that God gave you, which you can access anytime you want to learn to develop a Divine art.

CHAPTER 13

THE DEPARTED, AURAS, AND HEALERS

A few years ago, several people close to my mother and me passed away in a matter of months. The most devastating of them for me was my grandfather's death, and I put all my energy into trying to contact him. Unlike my mom, I don't easily speak with the departed . . . but my ability is getting stronger as I grow older.

The other day, for example, I was on the phone with a client named Tom. I kept getting a picture around him of a young man who seemed to be showing me something stuck in his chest. Finally, I described this figure to Tom, and he gasped and said, "Oh God, Chris—that's my brother, John! He was joking around, doing daredevil tricks, and fell and impaled himself through the chest on our fence." Not a pleasant story, but it gave Tom great comfort that I could determine John's identity and assure him that his brother was all right.

When my grandfather died, I started doing a meditative practice that helped me, and I'm glad to share it here. (But remember, you can also make up your own.) I'd visualize the 1,300-square-foot home where Mom raised us all, and then I'd add my own image of climbing up attic stairs. With each seven steps that I took, I'd visualize the light around me—very much like going through the tunnel— and one step at a time, I'd remember something about my grandfather: a saying of his, a look, a smile, the smell of his pipe, what he wore, where he sat, or an experience that we shared. When I'd get to the top of the steps, I pictured a small room to house our reunion. The first few times I tried this, I just got a warm, familiar feeling, but finally I not only saw him, but was able to talk to him as well.

Skeptics might say that this only happened because I wanted it so badly, or that it was my imagination. To hell with that! I know what I know, just as you'll be certain about what *you* see, hear, and feel if you try this exercise yourself. Besides, as my mother says, forget that damnable word *imagination*. With very little practice, you'll be amazed at how fast the images come and the wonderful sense you get that you and your loved one have really spent time together. Just remember to keep the white light of the Holy Spirit around you every step of the way, because it increases your energy and aura.

The subject of auras, by the way, drives many people crazy, including psychics. I believe what Mom always said (as did her grandmother before her): "Not everyone sees auras, and if they do, they might have cataracts." We've for years commented that it's more worthwhile to *feel* auras than to see them. We feel blue, get in a black mood, meet someone with a sparkling personality, and so forth. To be fair, a whole lot of "normal" people have seen a gold aura around my mom when she's onstage, and—believe me—I don't doubt them. Personally, though, I'd find being highly sensitive to auras disconcerting, and I hope that people don't doubt their own psychic abilities if auras don't happen to be visible to them.

Then there's the subject of healing, both in person and from a distance. Healers are psychics, and psychics are healers—whether they're dealing only with the mind or are involved in the actual laying on of hands. Please let me take this opportunity to beg you to be *very* careful about the "psychic healers" out there who take serious risks with their patients' well-being by supposedly performing surgery with their bare hands and no incisions of any kind. If a healer refuses to let a camera witness the operation or to let the material she claims to have removed from someone's body be examined by a legitimate medical lab . . . *run!* There have been some very real, very miraculous healers (including Stephen Arroyo and Padre Pio), but beware of anyone who tells you to throw away your medicine and follow *them*.

Healing is a transference of energy, and it happens in our office all the time. My mother and her ministers practice the laying on of hands with great results . . . but always in tandem with the medical community, and never as a substitute for any prescribed medication or treatment.

CHAPTER 14

LIFE WISDOM

If you've ever had a hunch, an intuitive feeling, or an uneasy reaction to a person, place or thing, then you've had a psychic experience. Keep remembering that *there are no coincidences*. That word is really taken from a mathematical term meaning "all sides meeting evenly"—which seems to be a far cry from the way we generally use it. It's similar to déjà vu, and many people confuse the two experiences. Actually, a feeling of déjà vu means that you've clicked into your chart and a memory has flooded over you—it could be a past-life memory, but is usually of the blueprint that you wrote before you came here.

I'm asked by almost all my clients what they can do to enhance the quality and spirituality of their lives, and one of my first answers is to live life in the present as much as possible. Tomorrow may not come, and yesterday is gone—all you really have is today. . . . What have you done now, today, this hour—*this minute*—to make the world a little better than it was?

Believe it or not, a great way to start making the world better is to learn to live with and love yourself. If you can exist in peace and harmony with yourself, then you can do so with others. We all know people who can't spend a moment alone, and isn't that a sad and exhausting situation? Aloneness isn't the same thing as loneliness—aloneness just means that you can read, write, listen to music, or just rest and shut out the world and be comfortable with that.

Start every morning with a positive attitude. Each day is new, and you can make it as positive or negative as you wish. Smile if it kills you—it'll make you feel better. Hum a tune. Give the day to God. Call a friend. Go out of your way to help a stranger. Be extra kind at work. Don't look for a fight, and don't feel that every slight is directed toward you. Compliment someone. Let another person go ahead of you in line or when you're driving. And most of all, surround yourself and everyone around you with the white light of the Holy Spirit. Every action has an effect. That's what karma really means: cause and effect.

Does this take much time? No, definitely not . . . it's a matter of minutes. Take five minutes to breathe and exhale, letting go of stress and negativity. Mentally put yourself on a mountain and look up at the stars, the moon, and the velvet night sky. Feel the breeze blowing through your hair. Ask your guide and your angels to attend you. It takes just a few moments to do this, and you'll feel refreshed and rejuvenated. It's a simple way to get your mind, soul, and body primed to be a vehicle for Divine knowledge—it's as though God and your God-center know that you're ready to pull the cord that lets all truth flow into you.

Your *life* can be a prayer. We hear about Jesus reciting prayers a few times, but he spent his three short years in public life *doing:* walking among the people, giving lectures, healing the sick, and being a comfort to humankind. No one faced more criticism and adversity, but he was full of love and knowledge, so he was brave and persevered. While prayer is important and a blessing of its own, the old phrase "Actions speak louder than words" really should inspire us every day of our lives.

CHAPTER 15

LOOKING BACK

When I was very young, I used to watch the parade of people coming into our apartment to get readings from Mom, and I remember thinking that what she did looked very confusing and exhausting. Frankly, I also resented having so many strangers around. But now that I'm a working psychic, I can experience for myself the "pull" that my mother felt back then and still feels to this day. As tiring as it gets, the rewards are constant and enormous.

I also have to admit that there are moments I'll always look back on and be forced to laugh—never at my clients' expense, but just at the range of ways we human beings find to express ourselves. For example, Andrea came into my office a few weeks ago and said, "Before we start, I want you to see me levitate" . . . after which she began jumping up and down, saying, "See? I'm off the ground!"

Maybe if she'd achieved some extraordinary height, I wouldn't have had such a tough time keeping a straight face, but the truth is that they were pretty ordinary hops. I finally ended them by simply saying, "That's very good. Now sit down and let's begin your reading." I focused primarily on directing her to one of the many wonderful doctors on our referral list, and I ended our session by refunding her money based on her promise that she'd get help.

I've mentioned before that there seem to be "coincidences" from one reading to the next, and the day that Andrea came in was no exception. Two clients later, a different woman named Justine calmly announced that she wanted to show me her backside, and she started to pull up her dress! On that note, I promptly stood up and said, "Please stop that—I'm not a doctor," and I had my secretary escort her out. I don't believe any psychic, or even a healer (without a legitimate license), can ever morally or ethically place his hands on—or look at—the bare skin of his clients, and I'll never betray that belief.

Although a lot of people switch jobs frequently, when a person's career involves helping others—such as being a psychic, healer, psychologist, or doctor—the commitment to it seems to be for life. I've particularly noticed this to be the case with legitimate psychics—I guess because it's so apparent every single day that all of our gifts and the information we transmit comes directly from God. Are some people better at it than others? Of course . . . it's like playing the piano or dancing. Studying, practice, and commitment make a difference, but nothing can take the place of a God-given gift to build from.

I've yet to meet someone who isn't tempted to get at least a quick glimpse into the future, no matter how afraid of it he or she might be. That curiosity has been around forever—all the way back to ancient people throwing stones or bones in search of reliable predictions or visiting the oracles at Delphi in classical Greece. Many famous and infamous leaders kept their own seers or astrologers on hand, from Napoléon to Hitler to even some of the early popes.

And then there are those people who get a little carried away in their eagerness for details about the future—something that I'm sure you've noticed if you've ever seen my mother on television. In the midst of questions about spirituality, missing family members, or deceased love ones, Mom will inevitably get someone who doesn't just want to know where the man of her dreams might be, but also his name, astrological sign, age, height, coloring, first and last name, and, if the person's really pushing her luck, his phone number. (This happens to me, too, as I explained earlier.) Mom and I both try to be very specific, but for heaven's sake, we're not *actually* God!

I don't deal with deceased relatives as frequently as my mother does, but the other day my client Brenda asked if I could contact her brother. Before I could even open my mouth to explain to her that this isn't my strongest area—poof! A spirit with a lanky build named George was standing in front of me with a tall woman named Maria. Before I knew it, along came Bernie and Anna, too.

I repeated all these names to Brenda in rapid succession as they appeared and introduced themselves, and she sounded almost bored or peeved when she replied, "Yes, George and Maria were my grandparents, and Anna and Bernie were my aunt and uncle, but I want to talk to my brother, Rick." If I were Brenda, I think that I would have been thrilled by this family reunion from the Other Side— or I would have at least asked how I could have possibly known those names. But no, this client was too focused on who *didn't* show up to truly appreciate who did.

What Brenda didn't realize is that Grandpa George might have a lot of helpful information to offer. Maybe he's the spokesperson for the group and has a message from Rick that he's eager to pass along. Why yawn at him or wave him away until she's at least heard him out?

Let's face it, though: If we humans weren't able to love each other in spite of—or because of—our peculiarities and keep a sense of humor about it, we'd all be (as Mom says) "out under some freeway overpass with our tinfoil and string collections."

These days we try to trick my mother into thinking that her life is more her own (as if she can be tricked that easily!). But the truth is, to this day she really is the camp-fire we all circle around as the sun sets. Eventually we head to our own houses (most of the time), but we just know the truth in our hearts: She is the anchor that keeps us from hitting the rocks.

We all went to Mom's lecture in San Francisco recently. I do love the excitement in the office before a talk, even the frantic rush and occasional panic over last-minute de-tails. One thing that I didn't mention earlier is the spe-cial bag that's always packed with Mom's lecture notes for every trip. I chuckle every time I see it because Mom has never looked at a note in her life . . . she just seems to like knowing that there's a bag full of them within reach.

As for the lectures themselves, she loves doing them. When my daughter was younger, she loved to go onstage and dance before Mom's entrance, oblivious to the fact that there were two or three thousand people looking on. But at the Palladium in Los Angeles, none of us was prepared when Willy, at two and a half years old and 50 pounds, made two simultaneous decisions: (1) that since Angelia had completed her interpretive-dance number and his Bagdah was at the mike, he should put in an appearance onstage as well, and (2) that his index finger in reality belonged inside his nose. (He wasn't picking his nose, I hasten to add—it was more that he'd found a hole in his face and thought he might as well fill it with his finger!) I swear that I tried to discreetly corral him away, but the instant he saw the lights and all those people, he decided—finger still in his nose—that he didn't want to leave the stage.

Angelia finally managed to lead him off, and Mom went on with her lecture . . . only to look up about five minutes later and find Willy standing behind her eating a doughnut. (Mom told me later that her agent, Bonnie, and her dearest friend, Lindsay, were in the audience tossing coins to see who got dibs to "just eat Willy right up," because merely hugging him and covering him with kisses never seems like quite enough.)

Speaking from my own perspective and knowing countless clients' experiences, I find that the time to start educating and encouraging children about their psychic gifts is when they're small, their memories from the Other Side are still fresh, and they haven't yet been made to feel self-conscious about their abilities. Don't dismiss anything as childish foolishness or tell kids that their imaginary playmates don't exist. Those "pretend" friends 99.9 percent of the time are spirit guides who are there to help. Particularly with children between the ages of two and four, it's best to ask questions and listen carefully and patiently to their answers.

When the phone rings, casually ask your kid who he thinks is calling. Even if the answer's vague—such as "a man"—notice how often he's right, and appreciate it rather than being discouraging. Ask him point-blank (but again, casually): "Where did you live before? Who were your mom and dad? What did you do for a living?" You'll learn volumes from the answers you get, as long as you remember to take them seriously.

Children in India, where the fact of past lives is accepted without question, can easily and comfortably discuss another life in a nearby village, and when they're taken there, they recognize their former homes and even their family members by name.

If your child has night terrors, ask her during the day what it is she's afraid of. No matter what she answers, again, don't dismiss it. For example, let's say she says, "I'm afraid of spiders." Don't say, "Oh, spiders won't hurt you," or "You're afraid of a little thing like a spider?" Instead, ask, "Did a spider hurt you before? Where? What happened when the spider bit you?"

In fact, a recent client named Veronica had a four-year-old son who was so terrified of spiders that it was actually disrupting the lives of everyone in the family. As my mother's spirit guide Francine says, "If you ask, you will get an answer." So I posed the questions I just listed to the four-year-old, and it turns out that in his most recent past life in Brazil, he'd died while a child from a tarantula bite. The boy was still carrying that memory into his new life, and Veronica was able to release it like a bad dream when she kept repeating to him, "That was then—you've had that life already. That's not going to happen to you again in *this* life, so you don't need to be afraid of spiders anymore."

So if the mind can travel backward, then can it also travel forward? Of course, it can—after all, in God's reality, everything is "now."

☆ ☆ ☆ ☆ ☆ ☆

CHAPTER 16

PRAYERS

My surroundings and my mother's definitely reflect our priorities. My office is smaller than hers, with a large desk, two pictures on the wall, a window, a plant, and—of course—photographs of my children. She has a larger office with a smaller desk, pictures, angels, a chiming clock, her father's ashes, mementos from her grandchildren, and favorite presents from clients. She's a collector, and I'm more streamlined, but I do think that my mind tends to be busier than hers, so my environment has to be sparse.

A typical walk-in day can get pretty hectic at our office, but Mom does a better job than I do of staying on a schedule. I usually run late, so clients invariably start "stacking up" in the waiting room. And more and more these days, people are stopping by just to look around, buy a book, or get an autograph.

After our morning clients, we take a half-hour lunch break, but even when we don't—contrary to a popular misconception—one reading never "blurs" into another. Each client is equally important, and any problem or issue that's troubling him or her gets our full, undivided attention. In fact, the more I let myself realize that these are very real people we're dealing with—with very real lives, fears, hopes, and pain—the more humbled I become. Thinking about them too much can almost make my clients' problems seem bigger and more overwhelming than I can handle, which is why I make such a point of maintaining a variety of interests, with my children always and forever my number one priority.

Like Mom, I always need an hour or so at the end of each day to get back to normal, and I always start every day with prayers for protection against the negativity that surrounds us all, no matter what our career or lifestyle is. My mother has her own set of prayers and encourages people to make up their own. I use three different prayers, which I always precede by surrounding myself with the white light of the Holy Spirit. I'll happily share them with you in the hopes that you might find them useful as well:

> *Dear Mother and Father God,*
> *Make this a day when I am pure of heart and motive and only speak Your truth, which comes through me from You. I ask that my power source as Your reporter be clear and without any reward to my ego or myself. I also ask, dearest Mother, that You keep Your mantle of protection around me.*

Dear Mother and Father God,

Let the Christ consciousness be alive in me this day. Let nothing detract me from Your holy will. Let me be a vessel for Your word and bring others peace, closure, and truth.

Dear Mother,

Keep me under Your sword of protection. Keep the white light of the Holy Spirit around me so that it deflects all negativity not only from me, but also from all the lives I have touched or ever will touch. Help me to increase in my spirituality every day. Let me grow in constant knowledge. Keep me on my chosen path to help and comfort. I ask this in Your name, and God's holy name, and in the Christ consciousness.

These prayers may seem simplistic, but they've always worked for me. They've seen me through depression on dark days; renewed my energy on sluggish days; and helped speed my recovery from colds, the flu, and bodyaches. They're not a cure-all, but the belief in God combined with your own will can create miracles, as I've seen time and time again.

I can't encourage you enough to create a calm place for yourself where you feel comfortable and at peace, even if it's just a chair in a quiet corner. Then simply light a candle and say your prayers. (Use your own or mine.) They'll help you ascend to God, to His will, and to your own ordained chart.

I certainly don't have time to meditate for hours—I don't know anyone who does, and I'll bet that you don't either. But just 10 or 15 well-spent minutes can help enormously. Pray quietly, being sure to take deep, cleansing breaths, bringing plenty of oxygen to the brain to clear out the cobwebs. Ask for protection and to be pointed toward your chosen path, and watch the positive changes appear in your life sooner than you might expect.

And whether you devote those minutes exclusively to prayer or add exercises toward improving your psychic abilities, don't forget to ask for the help of your guides and angels. As you're probably already aware, your guide is a spirit whom you knew on the Other Side who's trained to help you, study your chart, and communicate with you as your life's constant partner from Home. I can't tell you how often Mom and I have told a person his guide's names, only to hear, "You're kidding—I've always loved that name!" or "That's what I was planning to name my child or my new puppy."

No, your guide is not someone you know from this life. Yes, you do have loved ones around you all the time, not only from this lifetime, but from many past ones as well—but they're not guides. You and your guide were together before you were born into this life. And there's a very good chance that you've been a guide yourself or will be one in your eternal future on the Other Side.

Your guide is that small voice inside that you may have called your "conscience." My guide, Charlie, doesn't help me with my clients, nor does Francine help my mom with her readings. But we regularly ask them to help keep our channel clear and let God's knowledge as recorded in the Akashic Records be available to us. I fondly and respectfully think of guides as Divine window cleaners or the Drano that keeps information flowing freely into and through us.

Angels, on the other hand, are our protectors along the way. They never speak, but can imprint knowledge of love, guidance, and warnings. With the advent of the new millennium, we're seeing an upsurge in the belief in these wonderful beings that have always been around, but were sadly ignored for many years. All religions embrace and adore angels, but Catholics have a prayer to them that I especially love:

Angel of God, my guardian dear
To whom His love commits me here
Ever this day be at my side,
To light and guard, to rule and guide.

So, we're never alone, and they (the loved ones and heavenly entities who are watching over us) are waiting to show us the way and to infuse us with knowledge so that every one us, no matter what our life's work, can be a messenger of God's word. Whether that word comes in a dream, a flash, or a feeling, when you know that it's from Him, go with it.

CHAPTER 17

HEARING GOD'S WORD

If you embrace prejudice and dogma; if you can't keep your own opinions, anger, and hostility to yourself and in check; if your motives are anything less than pure; or if you can't remain nonjudgmental, you'll never be a genuine psychic—I don't care how gifted you are—let alone a successful one. The information that you're given is guaranteed to be clouded and scrambled by any inability to keep your ego and negativity out of the way. As my mother says, once you've opened yourself with a simple "Hit it, God!" you truly have to stand back, let go, and let God.

I know that when I'm not careful and don't take time to protect myself with the white light of the Holy Spirit, I run the risk of getting too involved in world problems; humankind's inhumanity to itself and animals; petty nonsense like bills, car trouble, or slow traffic; and general negativity to be able to hear God's word with the clarity and reverence that He deserves.

I received a letter a few days ago that read: "Chris, I really want to be more psychic, but I'm too caught up in the negativity of the world and how God can allow it." He only "allows" it by giving us the freedom to write our own charts before we come here and then learn from our experiences for the progress of our soul. Through the use of our psychic gifts, we can gain access to our clients' charts, help clarify them, and remind people that all of us came here to experience some negativity in order to learn and grow—for ourselves and for Him.

I can't reiterate enough, by the way, that a psychic has a tougher time gaining access to a chart without the consent of the person who wrote it. We don't just walk around reading any- and everyone on the street, nor would we want to. If you don't give us permission to "enter," we can, but it's harder to do so. That's why skeptics and negative people are harder to read, and clients who've been dragged to our offices against their will are also difficult. Mom will tackle those people, but I won't—it's too tiring. Does that mean that you have to be completely convinced before you walk in the door? Absolutely not . . . I'm just saying that anyone who's going to automatically shoot down everything that I say is too exhausting for me to deal with. I'll happily and quickly give them a "bless you" and a refund.

The Aborigines in Australia are among the most psychic people in the world, and they actually set aside a regular part of their schedule for what they call dreamtime. They live simply—which I'm convinced is more conducive to psychic phenomena than the complex world of "modern society." The Aborigines use their early-morning dreamtime to elevate their spirits. Inspired by them, I've developed the habit of setting my alarm for 15 minutes earlier than I have to get up. When I first started this, the temptation was to simply fall back asleep—but with time, training, and a conscious command to my mind before I went to sleep, I was finally able to let my mind go and send it to the stars, asking that it bring back God's energy and truth. It's a simple exercise that you can easily do, too. Program your mind in that quiet time for what you want to accomplish during the day . . . not the mundane errands, but the good that you can do, the peace and harmony that you can bring to yourself and others, and any especially difficult activities you face that you need Divine help with.

Mom still talks about how much she earned from the Samboro and Masai when she traveled in the Kenyan bush. Like the Aborigines, the people of this region practice their spirituality very quietly and internally, especially at sunrise and sunset, when they sit in silent dignity. For such supposedly "primitive" people, they probably know a lot more than we do. Can you imagine "civilization" growing still at dawn and dusk and treasuring as a blessing from God every flower, animal, and cloud—every tiny detail of this amazing world we all share? We'd all live much happier, more meaningful lives, I'm sure of that.

There's so much to learn from our connection with nature (a fact that these tribes who live "simply" seem much more aware of). Take animals, for example: They can anticipate earthquakes and other danger, grieve for each other, and will spot a spirit in the room in an instant. Civilized society calls this "animal instinct"—I say that's just a way to avoid acknowledging that animals are the purest, most psychic treasures on this planet.

CHAPTER 18

LEARNING FROM THE GIFT

Psychics, unlike almost every other professional group, never seem to hold conventions. I think that part of the reason has to do with the jealousy that some psychics feel toward each other (which I've never understood). I guess the more conventions we attended, the less we'd be out helping people, but there could be so much wisdom shared and so many healing breakthroughs worked out together, so I'm a little sorry that we don't all meet up every few years or so to make a positive difference as a group.

Look at how much people have learned from reading Edgar Cayce's work. He and my mom (to the best of my knowledge) are among the very few psychics who've made a habit of keeping all trance records, casework, research on past-life regressions, and so on. It's a shame, because so much could be gained if everyone stopped trying to be the only one who's right and threw away the ego nonsense. We could all move toward a general, psychically spiritual truth.

I envision a day when all of society will open up and proudly develop a sixth sense. The third eye will open with a bang, and everyone will be able to help one another by having access to each other's charts. Learning will become a favorite pastime because we'll have a greater understanding of *why* we're doing it. Human beings will no longer walk in the darkness of this life, not knowing where they came from or wondering why they're going in a particular direction.

I'm so proud of my mom for her elevating the word *psychic* to a soaring spiritual level. She's profoundly demonstrated that the worlds of psychic phenomena, religion, prophecy, and spirituality don't just coexist—they're very closely related.

So, knowing the probability that you were born with some form of psychic ability, don't suppress or be frightened of it. Suppressing it can lead to illness, depression, and exhaustion; and being afraid will only cause you to hide from your power, when you can instead greatly benefit from embracing and studying it.

My mother has often told the story of the first psychic experience that she can remember, when as a tiny child at a large family dinner she saw the faces of both her great-grandmothers melting. The sight terrified her, and when they both died a few weeks later, at first she actually believed that somehow she'd caused their deaths with that horrifying vision. But since her psychic grandmother, Ada, was there to help her understand what she'd seen, Mom didn't turn her back on her gift in favor of a more "normal" life—instead, she kept at it until she learned to use it to make an incredible difference. What a loss it would have been for all of us if she'd let herself be scared away!

Developing your own psychic gift can have more of an impact than you might imagine, whether you decide to earn a living at it or not. The more intuitive you allow yourself to become, the more you'll be able to explain to people why they chose the path that they're on, what they're learning by experiencing it, and why they charted the specific joys and tragedies that they did.

CHAPTER 19

THE OTHER SIDE AND ASTRAL TRAVEL

My mother and I discourage people from booking readings too frequently. Please don't take it personally—it's just that we have a horrible fear of people becoming too reliant on us (or on any psychic). We think that dependency and addiction are too closely related, and we don't want to be anyone's addiction. With the exception of major crisis situations, frequent readings shouldn't be necessary if the psychic has done his or her job and covered your general life path, along with a few specifics to keep an eye out for.

There are variables, of course, but your chart is essentially carved in granite. You wrote it of your own free will when you prepared to enroll in this school called life, and you take your charted courses—no matter how hard they are—or you don't graduate. Even if you don't, though, you can enroll in another life—not just to finish your previous lessons, but to sign up for new ones as well.

You can make a big difference for yourself and those around you by developing your psychic gifts and learning how to get in touch with deceased loved ones. Although I rarely make contact with people on the Other Side for clients, I'll do it much more often for myself, and it's brought me a lot of comfort. Here's the approach that's worked for me (and hopefully will for you as well):

Sit in your favorite chair and mentally surround yourself with the white light of the Holy Spirit. Make your body relax, starting with your feet and working your way up. Allow your breathing to be deep, calm, and rhythmic. Say to yourself: "I give myself over to God, so that He can lead me to my loved one." [In my case, that person is invariably my dear grandfather—my mom's dad.] *Keeping the white light around you, picture yourself in the midst of a velvet darkness and gradually begin to see a lighted pathway, iridescent with a bluish silver glow, leading into the heart of that darkness. Follow the path, noticing that you feel healthy and relaxed . . . but at the same time excited from anticipation.*

The path leads to a doorway. When you open it, the light inside is almost blinding, but as your eyes become accustomed to it, you're able to see that you're in a large room, with several people inside, some walking around, some sitting and talking to each other. You find a table, sit down, and wait. . . .

The first few times that I did this exercise, nothing happened. But on maybe the third or fourth try, my grandpa came and sat across from me at the table. He didn't say anything—he just smiled, looking young, healthy, and wonderful. I got a strong telepathic message that he was fine and happy, and it brought me a great sense of peace to know that.

I deliberately chose that large room for our meeting place because I knew that it's part of the Orientation Center on the Other Side, and it would be a natural place for my grandpa to find me. You can read more about the magnificent sights and spirits of Home in my mother and Lindsay Harrison's book *Life on the Other Side,* and in Mom's book *God, Creation, and Tools for Life.* (I'm not trying to do a commercial—it's just that both books are such great resources and the result of so many years of intensive research, and I'm very proud of my mother for writing them.)

The ability to do astral travel is obviously helpful in the exercise that I outlined. Astral projection has come naturally to me for as long as I can remember. Now you might think that this fact should make it easier for me to explain to you how to do it, but picture something that you've always known how to do and try to imagine teaching it to someone else. I'll do my best to explain, step-by-step, however, because it really can lead you to some great experiences.

Before you start practicing, choose a target location that you intend to explore—an easy, familiar place like your kitchen. Spend a few minutes meticulously examining your location to get your mind ready: Study the sink, the salt and pepper shakers, the design on the tiles—every detail, both large and small.

Once you've accomplished that, go to a quiet place where you can lie down without interruption. Slowly relax your body, starting at the feet and working your way up, and concentrate on your breathing until it's deep, calm, and rhythmic.

Next, project your mind into the room that you've just studied. This is a part of the exercise where you might get a bit spooked: When your mind/spirit is ready to take a trip away from the body, you'll often feel a vibration and a swoosh of air. Just keep remembering that you're in control. Before you stop yourself in fear, order yourself to let go with the simple word *release*. You might also find yourself looking down on your body from the ceiling. Again, don't let being afraid overwhelm you—you're in no danger. Just remind yourself to *release* again.

When you're more accustomed to the sensation of being outside your body, will yourself to be in your chosen room. As your mind is moving slowly through it, you might find yourself noticing even more details than you did on your physical tour of the room. You might also get the feeling that you're not alone, that your guide and angels are there protecting you, so ask them to show themselves. If they don't this time, consider it as something you have to look forward to on an upcoming astral trip.

Once you've practiced this exercise enough to get comfortable and know that you're always safe and in control throughout the astral journey, use the same method to go to the Other Side. (Don't worry, you won't die.) Mystics and other people going all the way back to ancient times have traveled back and forth from here to the Other Side on a regular basis to bring back knowledge—and they certainly didn't need drugs to accomplish it.

Eventually, ask to go to specific places on the Other Side such as the Hall of Wisdom or the Hall of Justice. I promise you that it will be a fascinating adventure. Above all, don't just waste this newly acquired skill by using it to wander around your own house all the time. Go visit a loved one on the Other Side or right here on Earth. Interestingly, many reported sightings of "ghosts" are actually just visitors on an astral trip saying hello.

You can read some fascinating material on this subject written by one of my mother's favorites, an early-20th-century medium named Eileen Garrett. (When I was a child, Mom often read to me from her book *Many Voices*.) On a test case, Eileen passed with flying colors under the strict supervision of doctors and researchers when she astrally traveled to a predetermined apartment that she'd never physically been to before. After 30 minutes, she was able to describe with total accuracy the half-cut apple she saw, the book on the table—including the page number and content it was open to—and every detail of the apartment that had been deliberately placed there by the researchers as a part of the test. It was a breakthrough for the psychic world, but it also helped explain a lot of supposedly psychotic experiences. The people involved in these weren't crazy—they were just taking astral trips without knowing it.

Mom has also done a great deal of research on this subject and has been a brilliant teacher for me and many others. Her knowledge in many areas is unparalleled, and she has a mastery of theology that surpasses most scholars. She recently did a benefit for a Judaic group in St. Louis, and the rabbi kept her for hours afterward to trade theological theories and perspectives.

A phenomenon that bears mentioning here is astral catalepsy, which is a form of paralysis during an astral trip. People in this state feel awake but can't get up, and they're screaming in their heads but can't make a sound. The reason for this is that the subconscious has been awakened, but the spirit has not totally reentered the body. If this should happen to you, make yourself relax and you'll come to. If you find yourself too frightened of catalepsy to try astral travel (as much as you might like to), simply surround yourself with the white light of the Holy Spirit ahead of time, and ask that when you reenter your body, you do it quickly, easily, and completely.

CHAPTER 20

TIPS FOR EMBRACING
YOUR ABILITY

Dreaming can be a great way of getting in touch with your power source or psychic ability. Just as I suggested that you do in your first waking moments (dreamtime), take five or ten minutes before you go to sleep to ask your guide and angels to assist your superconscious in reaching up to acquire knowledge—not only from your own chart, but from the Akashic Records as well—or in simply contacting loved ones while you sleep.

Lie down comfortably, and settle into a light, gradual relaxation. Hand your problems to God and the Universe and affirm: *During the night my mind is an open vessel to help me know the right solutions to these earthly problems.* Because remembering dreams and other answers that come during sleep can be unreliable, my mother also advocates affirming this: *I am able to access all records, keeping God's holy light around me. I also wake up at 3:30 A.M.* [or whatever time works for you], *take a sip of water, reach for the notepad and pen I keep by my bed, and write down a few key words from what I've just experienced during sleep.*

I remember one specific incident when Mom used that exact exercise several years ago. The question that she was seeking to answer while she slept was how she could spread the word, hope, and comfort of her theology to more people. She woke up at 3:30 A.M. as she'd asked, and the words *national study groups* came through so strongly that even though she was still half-asleep, she was able to retain them long enough to write them down. The next morning she looked at the pad of paper beside her bed and went into action, and her study groups are now thriving not just nationally, but internationally as well.

My mother has taught this technique to doctors, scientists, mathematicians—anyone and everyone who's struggling with life's problems, no matter how specific or general, or small or large. Program yourself to awaken long enough to write down the significant words, and you'll go promptly and soundly back to sleep. In fact, telling yourself that you'll go to sleep again after you've written down what you need to know will actually guarantee you a better night's rest. And the better you get at it, the more stimulated and invigorated you'll find your waking hours to be.

You can use this same exercise to help you overcome phobias or break unwanted habits, such as smoking, drinking, and overeating. Simply add this to your prayers: *While I'm asleep, help my superconscious inform my subconscious where to unplug the source of this phobia/habit so that I can dream it out into the open and release it.*

Rather than the waste of time we sometimes misjudge it to be, I believe that sleep can be very fruitful and quite meaningful. My mother's grandmother even believed (as does Mom herself) that we all travel to the Other Side during sleep three or four times a week, whether we're aware of it or not. Considering the clarity with which Mom and I and countless clients have been able to describe details of the Other Side (without exchanging any information ahead of time), I don't doubt this for a moment.

Mom was a reluctant psychic for many of her teen years, and I've had my moments as well, as I've admitted here. I think we've finally agreed that we weren't as reluctant about the gift as we were about the idea of not being able to keep at least one foot on the ground at all times. We're too practical to let ourselves become, as Mom puts it, "too airy-fairy." And my mother, like Houdini, is eager to expose any frauds or rip-off artists she comes across in this business. She's told me amazing stories involving beaded doorways, falcon wings, crystal balls, turbans, magic potions, and the like, and of her investigations that led to a lot of phonies being exposed and prosecuted.

I aspire to her courage for going after charlatans, bigots, cults, and other blights on a world that deserves so much better. Mom has always said that if she never accomplishes anything else in this lifetime, she'd love to help our profession become accepted, respected, and be the handmaiden to society that its true practitioners know it should be.

I hope that as you work toward developing your own psychic gifts, you'll make sure to learn along the way in order to give yourself a strong spiritual base. Study world religions; the Bible; and the volumes of material by and about other spiritualists, such as Sir Arthur Conan Doyle, Gladys Osborne Leonard, Arthur Ford, and Edgar Cayce. As my mother says, you don't have to believe each and every word that you read—you'll just be able to take with you what's truth for you and leave the rest. Even more important, you won't feel so alone or crazy (or both).

And be prepared for the probability that the more good work you do, the more dark forces will feel threatened by you and try to diminish your public light—whether your work is as a psychic or not. For example, Mom and I are constantly stunned by the bad and untruthful press that so many good people have had to weather. Montel recently went through this . . . I won't even dignify the press stories by repeating them here, but they proved that the media would much rather leap at an explosive headline today than take the time to arm themselves with the truth a day or two later. Montel has made countless contributions to society and keeps on making them, and I can say the same thing about Mom.

As a way of thanking them, if I could, I'd personally find a way to reward Montel and my mother with the perfect lives that they deserve. But, of course, just like the rest of us, they wrote their own charts, with their own built-in trials, tragedies, and lessons to learn. It reminds me of the old adage "The shoemaker's children don't always have shoes." The shoemaker (Mom's maiden name, by the way) is so busy making footwear for everyone else that his own children are the last to get any. To be honest, my mom is a lot more patient than I am about the rough spots in her life, but let a hardship come up in my life, my brother's, our children's, or Montel's—or in the life of anyone else she loves—and you'll see her throw the word *patience* right out the window.

Here are some tips on developing, embracing, and learning to celebrate your own psychic skills:

— Ask God and your guide to help you tap in to your passive memory, which is where all the information you need is stored. Repeatedly request that your words flow directly through you from God, and that you'll be able to articulate them as clearly and effectively as possible. Picture your power source as a perfect upside-down pyramid, like a funnel through which God's will can be poured into you.

— Ask that your intellect and emotion be cemented together in the ideal balance in order to be the most help to the most people.

— Remember that true psychics are always in league with God, not the devil, as was once ignorantly believed, and that there are no evil spirits to harm you, just lost souls who need your prayers to help them find their way Home.

— And never, ever let your growing psychic ability become so overpowering that you forget the ongoing importance of prayer!

Many years ago, Mom asked a dear doctor friend of ours how on earth he dealt with the occasional tragedy of a child dying. His matter-of-fact answer was, "I don't. I'll sneak back into a sick child's room when no one's around and lay on hands, pray, whatever it takes—because nothing but a cure is acceptable." And sometimes, between our friend's will, God's, and that of the child, he was able to accomplish that extraordinary phenomenon called a "miracle."

Prayer does work, believe me. Some of you might protest that you asked for a loved one's life to be saved and it wasn't, so obviously prayer doesn't really make that much difference. But what you're not seeing is that in a very real way, your prayers made a *big* difference: They helped you get in closer touch with God, and they helped your loved one go Home to the Other Side in greater peace. Just because prayers aren't always answered in the way you want doesn't mean that they're not answered at all.

CHAPTER 21

PAST LIVES

Like my mother, for a long time I resisted the idea of opening up the subject of past lives to people who hadn't experienced them on their own, because I avoid anything that even hints at implanting suggestions. But I've learned that leading people through their past lives can be an effective way of solving some very real present-life problems. It's an absolute fact that the truth will set you free . . . wherever it resides.

My mother's skill is far superior to mine when it comes to releasing phobias through past-life regressions. As she says, you can't tell lies to the subconscious: The spirit mind will always reject a false premise. But hit a valid chord and the soul will resonate with the truth, so the physical or mental pain can be immediately released.

Mom recently did a past-life regression show for Montel. One of her subjects was someone who had a terrifying recurring dream about black curtains on a window. Through regression, the woman found herself in London, in a life that ended in the horrible bombings of that city during World War II. (In preparation for the oncoming bombers, many Londoners covered their windows with black curtains.) Immediately upon waking from the regression, the woman could tell that her fear had been released and the dream would never happen again.

Another subject had a chronic phobia about being poisoned, to the point that she wouldn't drink out of anyone else's glass, or anything at all that had been left unattended. With Mom's help, she found her way back to two past lives. . . . In one, she had indeed died of poisoning. In the other, she'd died of stomach cancer, but it happened long before anyone knew what cancer was, and poison was the only logical diagnosis her doctors could come up with. After the regression on live TV, Montel offered the woman a glass of water that had just been sitting there, and she drank from it without hesitation.

Some of those anxieties that seemingly come from nowhere aren't from past lives, but from negativity you're picking up around you that has nothing to do with you. Start questioning yourself about your unease. Are you sure that it's coming from you, or could it be from someone else? Does it have a name, face, size, location, and so on? With practice, the question-and-answer method will help you pinpoint the exact source of your anxiety, so you can face it and do something about it once and for all.

Fear, as we all know, can limit you and separate you from other people and the joys that this world has to offer. So the more quickly you can get to the bottom of your fears and release them, the more freedom and happiness you'll have to look forward to.

Whenever you sense that you're in a place loaded with negativity, bless it in your own mind. Surround yourself and everything and everyone else with a blanket of the Holy Spirit's white light, and then watch how quickly all the tension and darkness in that location disappear in the healing glow of God's protection.

CHAPTER 22

A VARIETY
OF READINGS

As I've mentioned, I don't always see ghosts and spirits as readily as my mother does, but when she investigated a reported haunting at the Moss Beach Distillery for *Unsolved Mysteries,* Mom picked up four ghosts, and even *I* got a vision of the restaurant's notorious spirit, "The Blue Lady." We each did our own independent tour of the place and then met later to compare notes, and it thrilled us—as it always does—that our descriptions, sightings, and feelings were similar.

To any of you who are interested in going out on a haunting investigation or house blessing, I recommend that you do the same thing as our ministers do: Go with at least two or three other people; make a pact not to say a word during the entirety of the walk-through; and take notes on everything that you see, hear, and feel as you go along. Afterward, have an independent party transcribe all of your notes so that you can compare them and see their many similarities.

There's great variety in our life's work, no doubt about it. My first client one morning, for instance, was a man named Javier who was convinced that he was being harassed by evil spirits. Needless to say, he wasn't, and we were able to get to the real psychic core of his paranoia and eliminate it.

Mom later came out during a break and said, "Whew, what a day so far . . . a lost child, followed by an illness no one seems to be able to diagnose." As I headed back to my office, I heard her on the phone with a neurologist making an appointment for the client with the undiagnosed illness.

For some reason, on this particular morning I was thinking about the little physical quirks she and I have each picked up along the way. When Mom is into her deepest alpha state, you'll notice that she puts her thumbnail in her mouth. And I've found myself rubbing my forehead during really intense readings. It's almost as if we've found our own little cues to our psychic minds to go further, wider, and deeper for the client we're focused on.

Another of my clients that morning was complaining that sometimes she's her spirit guide named Sam, and other times she's herself—Samantha. I politely asked if I could meet Sam, and the woman immediately began speaking gibberish in a low, husky voice. When I asked for Samantha again, a bright, perky soprano voice came out in perfectly articulate English . . . definitely another candidate for a referral.

Then came a phone client, Marissa, who decided that she'd rather ask me test questions than get a reading.

"What do I look like?" she began.

I told her.

"Am I married or divorced?"

"Divorced."

"How many children do I have?"

"None."

This went on for a while until I said, "Look, I can keep this up as long as you want, but I'm not sure we're accomplishing anything that will help you."

Marissa wanted to ask just one more question: "Where's the bullet?"

I instantly answered, "It's in your head." Sure enough, she'd had a bullet lodged inoperably in her head for almost two years, and even though that was the only right answer I'd given that seemed to impress her, she was finally convinced enough to proceed with the reading itself.

Marissa was followed by Sharon, who only seemed to want to discuss where she'd meet her future boyfriend. I gave her a description of him, his first initial, the fact that she'd meet him on May 15, but all she kept asking was "Where?"

All I got in response to that question was a vision of her in the middle of the street. It made no sense to me, but those things aren't for me to edit or judge, so I said: "In the middle of the street."

It obviously made no sense to Sharon either, for she grunted a rather disgusted "Get real." However, I got an apology note from her a few months later. It seems that on May 14 she got a flat tire in the middle of an intersection, and Mr. Right—the exact man I'd described—came out of nowhere to help her. (Sharon was kind enough not to complain that I'd been off by a day. . . . You'd be surprised how often someone will try to invalidate an important prediction in which everything was absolutely accurate—it just happened at 2:30 instead of 1:30, or June 12 instead of June 2.)

I recently ran into a woman who introduced herself as Ingrid and reminded me that she'd gotten a reading with me 15 years ago and had been very disappointed. I'd told her that she'd adopt a blonde-haired baby girl and would relocate to Iowa for a while before moving back to California. At the time, she and her fiancé were happily living in California with jobs that they both loved at the same company, and they had no intention of leaving. They were also planning to have children of their own.

As it turned out, their company had transferred them to Des Moines, Iowa, for a couple of years to get some new offices up and running. Later, upon making the sad discovery that they were medically unable to have a child, they adopted a blonde baby girl, now a beautiful 14-year-old, to whom I had the honor of being introduced during our brief reunion on the street. Ingrid apologized for doubting me, but I was just pleased to see how beautifully her family's lives had worked out.

My mother and I were in a restaurant one night when a woman came running up to her and said, "Do you remember me? You told me to leave my husband five years ago. I didn't, and he cracked my jaw and broke my ribs."

Mom said, "Well, unfortunately, I can tell you what to do, but I certainly can't make you do it."

"You should have slapped some sense into me!" the woman replied.

Hearing this, Mom came right back with, "Apparently your husband finally did it for me." (Never hand my mother a straight line like that without expecting her to run with it. As she says, "We're not here to win popularity contests, we're just here to do good, love God, and then shut up and go Home.")

Of course, we also have to deliver difficult messages. It goes with the territory—and while it's part of our commitment, it never gets any easier. For example, at one of Mom's recent lectures, a woman stood up and asked, "Sylvia, how long will I live?"

Without hesitation, my mom answered, "Six years."

The audience groaned, but it was obvious when the woman said "Thank you!" that this was actually good news. It turned out that her doctors had only given her six *months* to live.

You'll often see my mother on TV or at lectures having to tell people that the missing loved one they're asking about is dead. I've had to do the same thing many times . . . it may look harsh, but the fact is that when these people cry (as they invariably do), the tears are more from closure, relief, and receiving confirmation of what they'd already felt on their own than they are from shock, grief, or disbelief. The truth beats false hope any day of the week, and the letters we get from those individuals weeks or months later have testified to that over and over again.

The hardest thing we deal with, no question about it, is the death of children. Even knowing that they charted such a short appearance on Earth for a reason and are happily back Home again doesn't lessen the pain in the families' hearts or the empathy we feel. This is one area in which I strongly disagree with many members of the clergy, who tell me that their response to parents is, "It's not for us to know why God took them." God didn't take these kids! Their spirits learned or taught exactly what they'd planned to, and—their work here finished this time around—returned to their full, busy lives on the Other Side.

CHAPTER 23

PSYCHIC QUESTIONS

Mom and I are blessed with good, close friends, and rarely do they ask us "psychic" questions. We'll talk about any- and everything, and every once in a while we might get a quick, "Will I get that job?" or "Do I need to see a doctor about this cold?" from one of them, but it's a fast yes-or-no answer and that's the end of it. It's no different, really, from any friend giving supportive answers to another.

I've never heard of my mother giving readings to her friends. If that were to happen (with her or with me), they wouldn't be friends—they'd be clients. I'm very grateful that no one close to us ever pumps us for information, and that includes our staff members and ministers. It's not some mandated taboo . . . it's just an atmosphere of "We love you two for who you are, not for what you can do for us."

However, Mom's been getting so much visibility these days that it's become more difficult to go anywhere with her. It truly never bothers her, and I try not to let it trouble me, but I do get concerned when people come running at her full force, getting right in her face to demand an answer to a question—even if we're in the middle of dinner or running for a plane.

Mom and I do compare notes on clients' problems, but we never, ever reveal their identities or otherwise breach their confidentiality. And it's fascinating how sometimes the same problem will come from a completely different source. A recent client of mine, Magdalena, was struggling with a weight problem, and I told her that while she needed a checkup with a doctor sooner rather than later, she should also address her belief (unknown to her until I said it out loud) that the bigger she got, the more armor she was building up to prevent people from hurting her. She promptly began losing weight after our reading. A client of my mother's was also struggling with a weight problem, but in her case, she'd starved to death in a past life and in this one was terrified of the possibility that every bite of food could be her last. Mom regressed her through that painful spirit memory, and she never had trouble with overeating or her weight again.

We occasionally get clients who have no present-life memories before the age of about eight or nine. From years of readings and consulting with many therapists we work with, we know that often those people are hiding a childhood trauma that their minds can't face. Locating the source of the pain through regressive hypnosis and then facing and releasing it with them is invariably effective, and depending on the gravity of the problem, we'll often find a therapist for the clients to work with for regular, ongoing healing.

Our files are filled with affidavits about how much we helped others feel better, conquer their depression, overcome chronic pain, and so forth. It's really gratifying, but you'll never hear either Mom or me claim to be a substitute for medical or psychological professionals.

✭ ✭ ✭

I had the best time the other night listening to Mom's stories about her grandmother Ada's interest in phrenology, which is the study of facial features, bumps, and other irregularities of the skull in order to detect various character traits. Some of the "facts" of phrenology seem almost worth a second look, while others are just fun. Grandma Ada didn't exactly ascribe a lot of credibility to any of this—she'd just be amused when one of the conclusions didn't seem that far off. I'll list them here in case you've never been exposed to them before:

People with . . .

- . . . a large, full mouth are very generous.

- . . . gums that show when they smile are very sensitive.

- . . . a high forehead are very intelligent.

- . . . a space between their teeth are very sensual.

- . . . a square jaw are stubborn.

- . . . eyes that are very close together are very suspicious.

- . . . small ears or a small mouth are very frugal.

And then there were Grandma Ada's home remedies, learned from her own mother in her native Germany, and by *my* mom at her beloved grandmother's knee. It's worth noting that my great-grandma told anyone who'd listen 60 years ago about an herb called Saint-John's-wort that helped lift depression. Now it's one of the great "new breakthroughs" in the health-food world.

My mother only remembers three more of these remedies:

1. Dandelion greens in spring ward off spring fever and malaise.

2. Collard greens prevent pinworms in children.

3. Asafetida keeps away diphtheria and whooping cough.

For a woman whose college degrees are in English and theology, my mother has an amazing ability to accurately diagnose physical problems. Since the psychic gene has been passed along through our family for 300 years, I've wondered more than once if Mom's inherent medical instincts might come from her great-great-grandmother, one of the first female midwives, who by the time she died was considered as qualified as any doctor around.

Not long ago, a woman named Bethany came in and sat down in my office, and before she said a word, I was immediately hit with the word *liver*. I asked her if she was having any discomfort on her right side, under the lower quadrant beneath her rib cage. She said that it had been tender but felt like nothing serious. That same word kept hammering in my head, until I finally said, "We'll continue this reading at another time. For now, we have to get you to a doctor for a bilirubin count."

Unbeknownst to Bethany until that rushed medical appointment, she had hepatitis C—and she started treatment immediately. I hope that you see what I mean about saying out loud whatever comes through to you, no matter how outlandish it might feel. It's better to be safe than sorry.

Mom and I usually aren't at all psychic about ourselves. But the other day, I hopped into the car to make a quick trip to the store, and the instant I got inside, I had a strangely strong sense of foreboding without any clue why. Usually I border on speeding down our hill, but that day I went very slowly. Sure enough, all of a sudden, one of my tires shredded and came right off the rim. Before I headed back up the hill to call AAA, I paused to acknowledge my guide out loud with a simple "Thanks, Charlie!"

A couple of nights after that, we were all out at dinner, and I noticed that Mom kept looking at the diamond that I bought her. I asked her what was wrong, and she said, "I don't know . . . I just feel insecure about my ring tonight."

About an hour after we went home, she called. She'd been getting ready to take a bath when she heard a "clink" and looked down to discover that the whole diamond and setting had fallen off onto the tile floor. We both paused for a moment to consider how easily it could have dropped onto the carpeted floor of the restaurant (which we never would have heard and might not have noticed). And yet, take note: We still don't play the lottery, and we never will.

Neither of us can answer the question "How do you do what you do?" any more than you can probably explain how you use the gifts you were born with. But even the people closest to us will occasionally be caught off guard and ask some version of that question. It especially makes me laugh when Montel will get confirmation of some answer that Mom had given on TV, turn to her with his mouth open, and say, "How did you know that?!"

She always rolls her eyes in a not-very-subtle *duh!* expression, and explains as if it's news to him: "I'm psychic."

To the people closest to us, we're "just us"—normal people with a not-so-normal ability—but it still surprises them when the gift "blurts" out something. I hope that someday it will become so common for everyone to develop their own psychic powers that the ability won't seem so abnormal anymore.

CHAPTER 24

LOOKING
TO THE FUTURE

Exercising your own psychic abilities is also exercising a new "muscle" known at the limbic (or "old") brain. Mom and the doctors whom she's done research with are convinced that it's this part of the brain that provides the "funnel" through which psychic information flows. Yet you'll never read a definitive explanation of exactly what the limbic brain does, which tells you how little we humans actually know about how our own minds and bodies work.

Francine, my mother's guide, says that she enters Mom's body through the right side of her head about an inch above her ear—which describes an area of the brain that's often referred to as the *dead zone*. So as you do the exercises described in this book, you might add a request to God that your channel be clear, and that the information be allowed to come through the dead zone or the limbic brain. I think that the more specific you can get, the more you're setting yourself up for success in developing psychically.

Remember that everyone who comes to you for psychic help will want specific answers, even when most of the time they're just a very sound yes or no. "Will I live a long life?" is a common question . . . but rarely does a client care about the exact age itself. Yes or no is almost always enough (although if they want to know the number, we can get that information, too).

As little psychic information as my mom and I receive about ourselves, we do know how long we'll each live: I'm going to reach just shy of 80, and Mom will be almost 89. (Any bets that she'll still be painting flowers on her toes until her last breath?)

I've been doing readings for 22 years now, and Mom's been doing them for 50. I hope that I've made it clear how much I love what I do, but I don't know if I'll have the stamina to keep it up for as many years as she has without the really long break that I have yet to see her take.

Mom's true love is writing. She's been doing it all her life and has won awards for it, but she never had the time or the financial luxury to fully explore it until her dearest friend, Lindsay Harrison, came along. Their first book was on the *New York Times* bestseller list, and their second one was equally successful—as were all the ones that followed—and I couldn't be happier for them or more proud of Mom. When you see them together, it's like they're joined at the hip, and the laughter is nonstop. One of their current mutual jokes is to be sitting around in their oldest sweats, Italian food ignored on the TV trays in front of them, their hair pushed back out of the way, and then sooner or later one of them will turn to the other and say,

"There's no doubt about it—we're definitely glamorous."
I know that Mom's dream is to continue her appearances,
do readings a couple of days a week, and just sit and write
with Lindsay until they're old and crazy.

CHAPTER 25

A SPIRITUAL
ANNIVERSARY

Tomorrow is Monday . . . not just any Monday, but the 20th anniversary of the founding of Novus Spiritus, my mother's Gnostic Christian church. There will be a big potluck dinner, and ministers and members of study groups will fly in from all over the country. Everyone else will say that we're celebrating the successful impact that the spiritual group has made on the world . . . but Mom will rejoice in the fact that we've all been together for this long without killing each other.

All kidding aside, there will be screams of joy when everyone sees each other again. There will be lots of prayers; a renewal of vows for the ministers; and then, inevitably, a board meeting that Mom will preside over to discuss budgeting, setting up classes and services, and the scheduling of who will be traveling with her on what dates. (The ministers rotate trips with her, and before going to any city, they set up regressive-hypnosis appointments, classes, and weekend seminars ahead of time.) But ultimately it will all boil down to our tight budget, which never seems to change . . . but wow, these people have done so much with so little.

Then it will be trance time, where Mom's guide Francine will use her body to share information with the ministers. I don't sit in on many of these: I'm not ashamed to tell you that I don't like the idea of my mother being gone while her body is still sitting there. Besides, I get dizzy watching her go into a trance because the thought of losing control doesn't appeal to me. (She feels the same way about astral travel, by the way—which, as I've made clear, I thoroughly enjoy.)

The ministers will pose a lot of questions to Francine about theology and spirituality, including issues that they've been asked to clarify by the cyberministry on the Internet. Cameras will be whirring nonstop, everyone will be taking notes, and it will be impossible to count the number of tape recorders running in that room.

The ministers will also be given the opportunity to ask Francine some personal questions. It's interesting to note how in the beginning, the group wanted to ask almost nothing but personal questions, but over the years, they've grown so much spiritually that their inquiries now almost never concern their personal lives, but have much more to do with specific ways in which they can improve their service to God.

CHAPTER 26

TRAVEL

Take it from me—traveling with Mom is an adventure than can lead you almost anywhere. I've been with her to England, Rome, Portofino, Monte Carlo, Paris, Barcelona, Greece and the Greek Islands, Mexico . . . I'm getting tired just thinking about it.

No matter where we go or what the national language is, there's some universally recognized spiritual-psychic-Divine light in my mother's eyes, so even people who've never heard of the United States—let alone Sylvia Browne—will approach her with something bordering on reverence. I guess psychics sing the song of the ages and sages.

I remember this lady in Lindos, on the Greek island of Rhodes, who carried her infant son to my mother and asked her to put her hands on his head to make him well. Mom did so, and managed to assure the woman with gestures and a few awkward words of Greek that her son would be okay.

This phenomenon is more pronounced in Egypt, and even more so in Kenya, where people literally start following my mom around calling out questions, without her being introduced to them as anything more than just another American tourist.

One of our favorite things about traveling throughout the world is the heightened sensory experience it provides and the richness of history that allows us to tune in to our surroundings, see what we can psychically pick up on our own, and then later conduct research to validate anything and everything that we've detected.

Of course, you don't have to have a passport to explore history, including your own. I've felt it in the Jesse James Home in St. Joseph, Missouri; and in missions, old houses, and churches. Visit a variety of places and see what strikes some familiar chord in you even if you've never been there before in this life. When a location does so, see if you can get a sense of what that place's surroundings looked like in whatever lifetime you might have been there before. There are plenty of old maps and records that can help you discover if you're right or wrong.

Even new houses can carry a vibration—not only from their occupants, but also from the ground upon which they were built. And when that vibration feels negative, people leap to the conclusion that they must be victims of evil spirits from an old Native American burial ground or something similar. When it suits their purposes, people seem to use supernatural horrors to explain perfectly ordinary things—but when some truly positive paranormal event takes place right under their noses, they dismiss it as being crazy. Go figure!

We hear all the time about haunted boats, planes, hotel rooms, houses, and even cars. You can bless anything that you think might be haunted using salt, water, a white candle, and a crucifix: Simply walk around whatever it is you want to bless sprinkling salt and water until you've surrounded it, and then move inside the circle, carrying the crucifix and making the sign of the cross with the candle.

That process worked on a client of mine named Martha, who truly believed that an evil spirit was climbing into bed with her every night. I knew that there was no such thing, but as my mother says, if people believe something, you have to start by accepting that as their truth and work from there. If Martha had lived closer to us, I would have sent two of our ministers to help her. As it was, I could only recommend the ritual I just described. She tried it, and the "evil spirit" went away, proving once again that the mind is a really powerful thing.

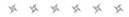

CHAPTER 27

A PSYCHIC'S LIFE

It's a new week. As I'd requested, Mom hands me her log of readings from the day before. Its contents are "typically" atypical:

- The death of a child

- A family needing clues and closure for an unsolved murder

- A couple divorcing, supposedly due to in-law trouble, but actually for deeper reasons

- A health problem that no one can seem to diagnose

- An older woman whose husband has passed, and she wants direction from him

- A stolen watch, ring, and bracelet

- The passing of a precious animal

- A woman who's afraid she's been cursed

- An ex-priest who's frightened that he's doomed to an eternity in hell

- A man with AIDS who wants to know how much longer he has left

No names are attached, and no clues to any client's identity ever appear in our logs. Our confidentiality is absolute, even between each other.

Mom's reading schedule continues throughout the year, with sporadic breaks for on-the-road lectures, classes, spiritual salons, media appearances, and church functions. When these activities interrupt her schedule too much, she begins to worry about expenses. It's then that we hear her yell out from her room: "Michael, book more readings for me!"

My mother's been saying that to him for more than 20 years, and he's always responded by groaning, "Go ahead—kill yourself." The fact is, she wears out both the staff and the ministers. When she's on the road lecturing, I've seen them so tired that they're almost crying, while she's heading off to her next interview or to have dinner with a friend. It's not drugs—trust me on that point (she can't even take aspirin)—she's able to do it because of that Divine fire in her belly that's always driven her and always will.

My week's log goes like this:

- A woman with cancer who's afraid of dying

- A young woman in pain because her boyfriend left her

- Another young woman who's in search of Mr. Right

- A man with a brain tumor, desperate to stay alive for his children

- A couple involved in a lawsuit against the state for flood damage

- A woman whose husband deserted her and their two children

- A man who has to find his father's will

- A woman struggling with guilt about not wanting to be around her family

- A young man in need of help making a career choice

- An elderly woman who'd like to know if her deceased husband is happy

When each day ends, Mom and I both need about an hour to make the transition from our readings to normalcy again. We both thank God that no matter what might be happening in our own lives, after our reading-room doors close, we've never once let it interfere with our full psychic focus on our clients (and I don't think it ever could).

After work, the whole family assembles, and we head out to dinner together to unwind. During Christmas, Mom cooks (she loves to do it, and she's great at it), and we sit around like a real family and talk. Eating out is nice—but nothing compares to staying in for a home-cooked meal. Angelia and Willy love to be home, too, although they've traveled with us so much that they're acclimated to just about anywhere.

At dinner, my mother and I may discuss a particular client whom we're concerned about in order to get input from each other, but again, no names. We share a chuckle over one of my morning clients: a man who wore chinos, a corduroy jacket, and a tie. As he sat down, I said to him, "You're a priest."

The man threw up his hands, visibly exasperated, and exclaimed, "Shoot! I just lost 20 bucks." It turned out he'd bet a friend that if he wore regular clothes to his reading, I'd never know that he was a priest. And he wasn't as upset that I'd found him out as he was that he'd lost $20!

After dinner, Mom and I spend time with the kids, and then I collapse into bed—while Mom does a four-hour radio interview. And the next day it starts all over again. . . . Isn't it exciting and glamorous?

And then there's my mother on the road: running for airplanes between readings and TV tapings, ordering room service, then racing for another plane and another lecture. In the first week of January this year, she hit four cities in four days before racing to New York to do six shows for Montel. That's glamour, too. Frazzled, tired, and not knowing where she was half the time because there comes a point where a hotel room in Cleveland looks a lot like one in Tampa, Mom still never once missed a chance to call home and check up on all of us.

So when people say, "I wish I had your life," I just sigh and agree, "Yes, it's very exciting." That's not to say for a moment that it really *isn't* great . . . I wouldn't trade it for anything. But I also wouldn't wish it on anyone who's just looking at it from the outside.

If you're thinking about becoming a professional psychic yourself, think about the time and energy commitment and the absolute devotion that it takes—and for God's sake, don't just do it for yourself. Support the people who support you and make as many services available as possible to give people options for how they can be helped, healed, spiritually counseled, hypnotized, and so on. Providing other people with a stimulating career is so important, and it's also gratifying to establish a place where so many people can come and get so many needs met.

As the world gets more disillusioned with all that's gone on before, with no reliable answers to its problems becoming apparent, people are in search of the truth more and more. I'm grateful to be part of that quest and committed to it. I want to do this for the rest of my life, and do it as well as I can, with excellence, and with God as my constant guide.

"Actually, I had been to numerous psychics, astrologers, and other readers in the past and really wasn't expecting very much, but I was delighted to find [Chris] far and away more intuitive about my life than any reading I had ever experienced."
— Becky, Texas

"I found my reading with Chris to be an eye-opening experience, especially with regard to my relationship. I was given so much more insight into the problems that I was having in this, and when I followed his advice, I was surprised how much better things got for me."
— March, South Carolina

"I had 50 questions written down before my reading. Chris was very accurate and answered nearly all of them before I even asked. He nailed my personality, my dead-end job, a residence move, a house in two-and-a-half years, my animals, and my partner. I also received very accurate answers to questions I had for friends and family members. I now have an exciting outlook for the future and relief for some major problems I had been dealing with. What a really cool experience!"
— Suzanne, New York

"Chris, the time we spent talking will be one of the most treasured and memorable moments of my life. You have no idea how much you helped me. I will be forever grateful to you."
— Reba, Georgia

"I made a complete recovery, as you predicted. I could not have gotten through this past year without you, Chris."

— Camilla, Florida

"It has only been a short while since my phone reading with Chris, and already things are occurring as he said they would. What a gift! I hope others will take the opportunity to let Chris help them as he has me. I will never forget the experience."

— Janna, Indiana

"Chris was very helpful in my life's journey. He told me of a man coming into my life, his physical description, and everything about him. Well, two weeks later I met this guy. He had the same job and description. I think everyone should get a reading if they feel even a little off track. You can spend thousands more going to a psychiatrist, but the difference with Chris is that he's someone who knows you from the start and tells you exactly what to do with your life that is always in your best interest."

— Kristina, Southern California

"I had doubts about my decision to retire next year and move out of state. After talking to Chris, those doubts disappeared. His insight into my life was amazing. I felt immediately so much better and more relaxed. I now feel I can go ahead with my plans with no apprehension. He told me exactly how to 'get the ball rolling.' My family attitudes were made so much clearer, and that was a great relief. I am now able to stop worrying so much and feel so relieved and more relaxed and at ease. The best thing I

ever did was to have a talk with Chris. I am so glad I contacted him. Thank you."
— Jackie, Nebraska

"Chris helped me to make a big decision and to move on from a situation in my life that had been holding me back. I am so thankful for it. He was very accurate about my health issues and work problems. Without his advice, I know I would be in the same standstill position I had been for the last five years."
— Ken, Missouri

"My personal experience with Chris was a very happy one. After losing my husband and almost losing my son, I wasn't sure where to go. I was afraid I wouldn't have anything to look forward to, but Chris put my mind at ease and gave me direction for my work and with a future relationship."
— Nancy, Florida

"My reading with Chris was very emotional for me. I've had many different types of readings but none like this. He told me over the phone about my life partner—things that no one could know without being a close friend or family member. He helped to ensure that I am on the right track for the future."
— Susan, New Jersey

"Chris was right on! I was on the other phone during my mother's reading, and he graciously asked if I, too, had any questions. He knew about my biological father, whom

I found when I was 27. Chris was so right on that it scared me. Thank you for this wonderful opportunity."
— Don, Oregon

"I had never spoken with a psychic. I was truly amazed at the accuracy of all the information that Chris covered. Since the reading and studying Sylvia's books, I now feel closer to God. This is perhaps the greatest gift I have been given."
— Doug, Colorado

"Chris is wonderful and put me at ease right away. He was so right about so many things, including my health issues and even so many small things I hadn't expected him or anyone to know. I felt so many emotions as he talked to me, and I came away feeling reassured and positive about the future."
— Vicki, Northern California

"The information Chris gave me was a perfect confirmation or mirror (if you will) of my life's path. It was a reminder to me of how precious and beautiful my life really is, plus a rich lesson in trusting one's own inner knowing and direction. His sincere, committed work is a light for humanity. His pledge and delivery of knowledge, words, and love are needed in our world."
— Darlene, Arizona

"Christopher accurately described various health issues occurring at the moment. He also described various personality circumstances I was dealing with. There is no way he could have known this information even by searching public records or asking me various questions, and I will add that he did not ask me a single question. He always stated everything very matter-of-factly. His voice has a presence of being very kind and caring. He makes you feel relaxed, as if you are speaking with a friend. All in all a wonderful experience."

— Carrie, Nebraska

"Chris did a reading for my husband last week. My husband talked to me regarding the things he mentioned to him about me. I would like to thank you so much for that. I have followed his recommendations, and I cannot believe the way I feel! I simply feel so energized, full of hope, and love. Thank you, thank you, thank you!"

— Jane, Washington

"I had the most awesome experience. Chris told me I would be moving in my reading, and this was shortly after I had purchased a very expensive new home. At first upon hearing this, I was very disappointed. Not too long after the reading, I was walking on a deserted beach, praying for an answer to a dilemma, when I was suddenly hit by a large wave. While cleaning the sand off myself, I noticed an old woman sitting on a nearby bench who just seemed to come out of nowhere. Moments earlier there was no one there. The woman said to me, 'You should listen to Chris.' I turned to finish cleaning off the sand and when I turned back around, the woman was gone. Shortly afterward, I had a lucrative offer for my home and subsequently sold it. Just recently I learned that the house I sold is within six feet of being washed away from its foundation because of erosion. I can't thank Chris enough for saving me from what could have been a very expensive hardship."

— Carol, Southern California

"Chris, everything you told me in my reading has already come true. I am so pleased with your messages. You told me about my health, and it was completely accurate. You also described in great detail a friend I was going to meet, and I did, exactly as you described."
— Pauline, Arkansas

"I had a reading with Chris in March, and by November, everything he told me had come out just as he predicted. I still can't believe how accurate he is."
— Diane, Pennsylvania

"I am so pleased with both of the readings I have had with Chris. What Chris told me has given me such positive direction and answers I could not have obtained anywhere else."
— Marlene, Northern California

"This is probably redundant to say . . .'Chris was right' . . . but I wanted to let him know. I talked to him about my legal case concerning a motorcycle accident. It really helped to know this information and keep calm during the mediation with the judge today. Chris was not only right on the issues, but also the money we settled on. Thank you, Chris. The information helped me keep my sanity these last couple of years."
— Debra, Arizona

"Chris literally saved my life. He advised me strongly to get help with my substance-abuse problem and recommended I be institutionalized, otherwise my life was in danger. I did so shortly after my reading, and found out just how close I was to death. Thank you, Chris, for saving my life."
— Lucy, Florida

"Chris told me that my brother, who had walked out of my life 20 years earlier, was still alive. Neither my mother nor I could believe this, since we had no word from him during all those years, and he had been declared legally dead. Even the police had given up finding him. He walked back into my life in August, and I was totally shocked. Since the reading, everything else that Chris told me has come out just as he predicted."

— Jan, Oregon

"I have never spoken with such a warm and yet professional psychic in my life. The added bonus was that he was so amazingly accurate. He could have simply made the predictions he did concerning my future, and I would have been overwhelmingly impressed. Yet he took time to give me advice and counsel me on some really difficult decisions I had to make. For the help and the peace of mind I received, Chris is worth ten times the fee I paid for my reading."

— Charles, Michigan

"God bless you, Chris, you are truly a miracle from God. You were just as awesome in my second reading as you were in my first. I am so completely impressed with your readings that I am giving my sister the opportunity to experience your beautiful gift."

— Sherri, Kansas

"Everything Chris told me turned out right 'on the money.' He is truly amazing. What a gift!"

— Richard, New York

"I am so sorry I argued with you, Chris. You turned out to be exactly correct on nearly everything I asked. I just couldn't see it at the time."
— Diane, Washington

"Thank you, Chris, for your amazing predictions and for sharing your gift. Just as you predicted, I did meet someone with the initials *J* and *D*, with thick, dark hair that's longer in the back, age 34, who lives approximately 20 minutes from me, has a son, and who has the same spiritual beliefs as I do. You also said this person had a lot to do with ships and working around water, which is exactly what he does. You were also completely accurate about my health and the health of my children. I am now getting help from my gynecologist on my female-organ imbalance; and as you suggest, my daughter is getting help with her bowel problem, which you also accurately predicted. Even more amazing, there was an arrest for the arson/ murder case I asked about. I want to thank you over and over again for sharing your wonderful gift with people like me. Many, many a night I prayed for help, and through you, my prayers were answered."
— Tilli, British Columbia

"Chris is amazing. Everything was right on. I was going through a time in my life when I needed a lot of questions answered, and he answered them all."
— Pat, Washington

"Chris was dead-on when I talked to him—to the penny. It was amazing."
— Anne, New Jersey

"Everything is falling into place that Chris told me about. He is really good!"
— James, Texas

"Thank you, Chris. After several years, my constant headaches have stopped. You were right about my needing glasses and that I had a problem in my third tooth from the back on the right side. This was exactly why I was having the headaches."
— Diane, Northern California

"Your no-BS answer to each of my relationship questions was exactly what I needed to hear. You were so right about all three of these people, and yes, I have been spinning my wheels the past three years hoping John would change and come around, and you certainly accurately predicted that outcome. As you advised, I am now going on with my life and looking forward to a new beginning and a brighter future than I would have ever believed possible."
— Suzanne, Idaho

"The year isn't even up, and so much of what you predicted has already materialized. How do you know these things? We've never even met, but I certainly hope we do one day. I felt like I was talking to an old friend whom I had known all of my life."
— Bill, New York

"Chris, you were so right on concerning my domestic situation and health issues, I swear it felt like you had been living in my house."
— Richard, Wisconsin

"Thank you for the wonderful readings, Chris. You have helped my husband and me in so many ways! I have referred so many friends and family members to you, which I do not normally do unless I am totally confident about someone."
— Paula, Florida

"Chris, your reading helped me in so many ways and afforded me the courage to make a major decision in my life that was long overdue. I have had numerous readings in my life, and the majority have been from people offering general information that left me feeling a greater lack when I left than before I sat with them, saying things like, 'You'll meet someone with the letter *P* in their name' (big deal). I used to wish I could find just one person who was 'for real' and on whom I could depend to tell me what I couldn't reach myself. One of my biggest disappointments was that Edgar Cayce went and died on me before I could meet him. And then I found you. Thank you very, very much. I just thought you should know how much your efforts are greatly appreciated and how much you help people."
— Catherine, New Jersey

"I would like to thank you from the bottom of my heart for the wonderful psychic reading you gave me. It helped me see what I must do to better myself and how I am keeping myself from being successful in so many areas by living in the past. You are awesomely accurate and a very sincere, loving, and caring individual. I will never forget our session together. I have changed my life for the better in more ways than I can possibly ever tell you."
— Kenneth, South Carolina

"You were exactly right about my lawsuit, Chris. It was dismissed yesterday. Thank God. Thank *you*."
— Sam, Utah

"Thank you, Chris, for the timing of your call. It was miraculous to me. I was feeling scared earlier in the day, wondering how and when I would find strength in a Higher Power to help me through my relationship. After your call, I now realize I have that strength in God through you. You are like my guardian angel, and I feel blessed to have had you in my life when I most needed help. Thank you so much for being there and sharing your gift with me."
— Kim, Colorado

"I am ashamed to admit that I was one of those 'nightmare' people I'm sure your mother and you hate dealing with, who argues and shakes her head 'no' during the entire reading. What you were telling me during the reading seemed so far-fetched that I just couldn't possibly imagine how even half of the things you told me about would occur. Well, here it is a year and a half later, and everything has turned out exactly as you said it would. Boy, am I ready to eat a lot of crow, starting with my offering a sincere apology to you for ever doubting your words. God bless you, Chris, for your patience with me; your understanding of my skepticism; and most of all, for your wonderful, wonderful insight."
— Denise, Connecticut

"I just had to tell you, Chris, just how accurate you were in my reading: You were right about my kidneys—I was having a problem with them. As you suggested, I am drinking plenty of water and cranberry juice to keep them flushed, have consulted a physician, and am doing much better in this area. I did gain the weight, as you saw, and am trying to lose it now to help lower my blood pressure. My husband did get promoted, as you saw, and you were so right about my daughter. She was not happy in her marriage. She did separate from her husband, and they have since worked things out and are now back together. Thanks so much for all your help."

— Rose, Alabama

ABOUT THE AUTHOR

Chris Dufresne, the son of psychic/best-selling author **Sylvia Browne,** is a highly respected psychic in his own right who has been in practice for more than 20 years. Chris, who inherited not only his mother's significant psychic abilities, but also her writing talent, is the author of *My Life with Sylvia Browne* and works alongside her in the Northern California area. He has appeared in a featured article in *People* magazine, and has also been profiled on TV in *Bay City Limits, Northwest Afternoon,* and the *Montel Williams* show. He's the father of two children, Angelia and William, and is very proactive in all of their school and extracurricular activities.

NOTES

NOTES

NOTES

NOTES

NOTES

NOTES

We hope you enjoyed this Hay House book. If you'd like to receive
a free catalog featuring additional Hay House books
and products, or if you'd like information about the
Hay Foundation, please contact:

Hay House, Inc.
P.O. Box 5100
Carlsbad, CA 92018-5100

(760) 431-7695 or **(800) 654-5126**
(760) 431-6948 (fax) or **(800) 650-5115 (fax)**
www.hayhouse.com® • **www.hayfoundation.org**

Published and distributed in Australia by: Hay House Australia Pty.
Ltd. • 18/36 Ralph St. • Alexandria NSW 2015 • *Phone:* 612-9669-4299 •
Fax: 612-9669-4144 • www.hayhouse.com.au

Published and distributed in the United Kingdom by:
Hay House UK, Ltd. • Unit 62, Canalot Studios • 292 Kensal Rd.,
London W10 5BE • *Phone:* 44-20-8962-1230 • *Fax:* 44-20-8962-1239 •
www.hayhouse.co.uk

Published and distributed in the Republic of South Africa by:
Hay House SA (Pty), Ltd., P.O. Box 990, Witkoppen 2068 • *Phone/Fax:*
27-11-706-6612 • orders@psdprom.co.za

Published in India by: Hay House Publications (India)
Pvt. Ltd., 3 Hampton Court, A-Wing, 123 Wodehouse Rd., Colaba,
Mumbai 400005 • *Phone:* 91 (22) 22150557 or 22180533 •
Fax: 91 (22) 22839619 • www.hayhouseindia.co.in

Distributed in India by: Media Star, 7 Vaswani Mansion,
120 Dinshaw Vachha Rd., Churchgate, Mumbai 400020 •
Phone: 91 (22) 22815538-39-40 • *Fax:* 91 (22) 22839619 •
booksdivision@mediastar.co.in

Distributed in Canada by: Raincoast • 9050 Shaughnessy St.,
Vancouver, B.C. V6P 6E5 • *Phone:* (604) 323-7100 • *Fax:* (604) 323-2600
www.raincoast.com

Tune in to **HayHouseRadio.com®** for the best in inspirational talk
radio featuring top Hay House authors! And, sign up via the Hay
House USA Website to receive the Hay House online newsletter and
stay informed about what's going on with your favorite authors. You'll
receive bimonthly announcements about: Discounts and Offers, Special
Events, Product Highlights, Free Excerpts, Giveaways, and more!
www.hayhouse.com®